G-D'S *Love Letters* A - Z

BY
JOSEPH B. GOLDBERG

Copyright © 2023 by Joseph Goldberg

All rights reserved, including the right of reproduction in whole or in part in any form without prior permission of the publisher, except as provided by USA copyright law.

All Scripture quotations, unless otherwise indicated, are taken from The Holy Bible, New International Version®, NIV®. Copyright © 1973, 1978, 1984, 2011 by Biblica, Inc.® Used by permission. All rights reserved worldwide.

Scripture quotations marked (NLT) are taken from the Holy Bible, New Living Translation, copyright ©1996, 2004, 2015 by Tyndale House Foundation. Used by permission of Tyndale House Publishers, Carol Stream, Illinois 60188. All rights reserved.

Scripture quotations marked CSB have been taken from the Christian Standard Bible®, Copyright © 2017 by Holman Bible Publishers. Used by permission. Christian Standard Bible® and CSB® are federally registered trademarks of Holman Bible Publishers.

Published by Joseph Goldberg
5640 East Amherst Avenue
Denver, CO josephb.goldberg@gmail.com

Cover design: Terry Dugan
Editorial Team: Marcus Costantino, Mark Tuggle, and Penny Tuggle
Interior layout: Ben Wolf and Justin Shreeves

ISBN-13: 979-8-9886615-0-4
First Printing, 2023
Printed in the United States of America

*Dedicated to my dears: Olivia (Libby) and Lincoln (Link)
Learn the alphabet so you can know the Word of G-d.*

*I commit this to You,
Father G-d,
Brother Jesus,
and Advocate Holy Spirit.*

*Not my glory, but Yours.
More precious than gems, gold, silver, or bronze.
The Trinity is the truest treasure.*

May it bear Your fruit and testimony in Jerusalem, Judea and Samaria, and to the ends of the earth. Amen.

G-D'S *Love Letters*

A - Z

BY
JOSEPH B. GOLDBERG

Almighty Abba the Author-ity

Jesus calls G-d "**Abba**," His "Father" in Hebrew. He is "Lord G-d, who is and who was and who is to come, [G-d] **Almighty**," whose breath authored all, like Scripture, and granted all heavenly and earthly **authority** to Jesus. Only Father, You shower us with countless gifts like compassion, loving discipline, comfort, and protective *angels*. But best of all, You love most to call us your children. Love You, Pops![1]

Alphas

G-d and Jesus are **Alphas** (**A**- the Greek alphabet's first letter), present "in the beginning," "before the ages began," and "from ancient days," co-creating everything. Jesus said, "Before Abraham was born, I am!" Abraham rejoiced at Jesus' future humanity, the Incarnation. G-d and Jesus are there always, even if not physically.[2]

Anchor, Answerer, Advocate

Life's waves crash down, tossing us to and fro. Cling to hope, the souls' **anchor**, secured by G-d's unchanging

---

[1] Mark 14:38, Revelation 1:8, Matthew 23:9;29:18, Galatians 1:24, Psalms 91:11;103:13, 1 John 3:1, 2 Corinthians 1:3, Proverbs 3:11-2, Hebrews 12:7

[2] Genesis 1:1, 2 Timothy 1:9, Isaiah 43:13, John 8:56-58

oaths. He sent Jesus, the only **answer** to humanity's most dire dilemma: our fractured relationship with G-d. Jesus foreran us into the heavenly veil, the holiest of holies, as our anchor. He made Himself the missing piece ✥ to our spiritual puzzle, the lone path back to G-d. Jesus is our **Advocate**, pro bono! He is our "Wonderful Counselor" who keeps His loving eye 👁 upon us. Jesus will represent us on our heavenly court date when we stand before G-d's seat of judgment. With sinful charges brought—every careless word—Jesus will substitute His impeccable record for our tarnished rap sheets because He nailed our legally demanded debt to the cross. Until then, G-d and Jesus sent a permanent Advocate, the Holy Spirit. Loving litigation![3]

Anointed Apostle of Atonement

Anointing is ceremonially applying oil on an object or leader to confer holiness. Jesus was different. He was anointed with the "oil of joy," the Holy Spirit, and His Father's power. G-d sent His Anointed messenger, the first **Apostle**, to create the gospel: the good news that Jesus willingly laid down His life, in loving obedience to His Father's commands, to appease His wrath 😣, **atoning** for all of mankind's sins forever—mine and yours. G-d also anoints those in Jesus.[4]

Apocalyptic Avenger: Amen!

Don't waste time ⌛ seeking earthly justice—and forget Iron Man! Jesus will **avenge** all wrongdoings like fraud, oppression, sexual immorality, and murder. Just love, even those who harm you. With the **Apocalypse**, we will see

---

[3] Hebrews 6:19-20, John 14:6;16, 1 John 2:1, Isaiah 9:6, Colossians 2:14, Matthew 12:36, Ephesians 4:14, Romans 14:10, Psalms 32:8

[4] Isaiah 61:1, Psalms 45:7, 2 Corinthians 1:21, Acts 10:38

things properly through G-d's eyes; G-d's mystery will be revealed. We will see true right from wrong. Vengeance will be His.

"**Amen**" in Hebrew means "I absolutely agree 🫶," and its root is related to the words for "faith" or "belief." Jesus calls Himself the "the Amen" because He is the one to believe and have faith in. We can rest easy. All will be repaid justly. "For all the promises of G-d find their 'yes' in [Jesus]." Through Jesus, we utter our "amen" to G-d for His glory.[5]

---

[5] Leviticus 19:18, Romans 12:29, Revelation 3:14, 2 Corinthians 1:20

Banner & Bridegroom

"Neis" is Hebrew for **banner**. Moses named his altar "Yahweh is my banner." While fiery serpents killed many Israelites for bad-mouthing G-d, G-d answered Moses' prayer, instructing him to make a fiery bronze serpent on a "banner ⚑." Anyone bitten was healed just by looking at it. The earth swallowed and burned Korah and his rebellious cohorts as a warning sign. King David said that G-d gives those who fear Him a banner to display. Isaiah prophesied of a "banner of the peoples," who will whistle for all to gather from the earth's four corners. Jesus is our banner: the flag raised to the world with which we identify ourselves, our ideals, and our principles. It declares our healing source, calls to fight oppressors, but warns against a fiery death.

Jesus is our banner, but we are also the bride to His groom, or **bridegroom** 🤵. "In that day," declares Yahweh, "you will call me 'my husband,' you will no longer call me 'my Master.'" John the Baptist said he was the friend awaiting the bridegroom, Jesus, full of joy when He came. Jesus calls His disciples the bridegroom's attendants, who would fast at the right time, after the bridegroom was taken. Paul wrote of his godly jealousy for the church, having promised the church to one husband, to Jesus. Lastly, marriage between a husband and wife is given as the model of Jesus giving Himself up for His church—both eternal vows.[6]

Beloved Baptizing Brother & Bread

Father G-d said of Jesus, "This is my **beloved** Son, in whom I am well pleased" during His baptism. Repenting with **baptism** is why Jesus is unashamed to call us His **brothers** and sisters; we become beloved and holy children of G-d, like Him—the same family. The Israelites were baptized into Moses in the cloud and the sea. John the Baptist baptized with water and repentance. Jesus baptizes in the Holy Spirit and a testing fire—brothers and sisters are born through adversity. We appeal for clear, faithful consciences to the Father's will. Buried underwater, dead to sin like Jesus, then rising again, like His resurrection, we are spiritually reborn anew and clothed in Jesus. We are born of living water and one Spirit in the names of the Trinity. *As bathed* souls, meriting nothing, we are mercifully gifted the Holy Spirit in grace—our spiritual adoption papers ◾ as Jesus' siblings and co-heirs to our heavenly Father's kingdom.

    Bread 🌾, like baptism, was birthed in cursed affliction but became a gift of holy, life-giving salvation. Original sin's curse brought toil to sustenance: "By the sweat on your face, you will eat bread." Passover—Yahweh's Festival of Unleavened Bread of Affliction—commemorates Israel's enslavement in Egypt ending hastily after Jesus delivered them. Manna—G-d-gifted bread from heaven during Israel's desert travels—had a disclaimer: "Man does not live by bread alone, but by every Word from Yahweh's mouth." Then Jesus said, breaking bread at His Last Supper, "This is My body, given for you." Jesus' body gives the world life, but He is also G-d's eternal "Bread of

---

[6] Exodus 17:15, Numbers 21:8-9, John 3:14-5;3:29, Numbers 16:31-2, Psalms 60:4, Isaiah 5:26, Hosea 2:16, Mark 2:19-20, 2 Corinthians 11:1-2, Ephesians 5:25

Life" from heaven—life through death. The Lord's Prayer, "Give us this day our daily bread," requests physical food but more vitally, spiritual proximity to G-d. Jesus sustains both (physical and spiritual) when we make Him our eldest brother through baptism.[7]

Blessed Blessing

G-d promised Abraham: "All nations on earth will be blessed in your seed ♉." Jesus was that seed and the promise fulfilled. Jesus' death ended the futile ways of our forefathers and guaranteed G-d's blessing—His favor, protection, and entry into His kingdom. Jesus' blood purchased the freedom of the "kindred of G-d from every tribe, language, people, and nation." How? With the promised **blessing**, which is the Holy Spirit. Jesus had to ascend to heaven, to the right hand of His Father, so the Holy Spirit could come down to bless everyone. When the Holy Spirit reaches every nation, the end will come with Jesus' return.

Bless the Father who sent His Son to give every spiritual heavenly blessing. Blessed be:

- ✝ The poor in spirit, for theirs is the kingdom of heaven
- ✝ Invitees to the Lamb's marriage supper
- ✝ Those who faithfully believe but have not seen Jesus
- ✝ Those with pure, obedient hearts, for they will see G-d
- ✝ The peacemakers, who will be called "children of G-d"
- ✝ Yahweh's trustful, who will be firmly rooted and ever green
- ✝ The trialed steadfast
- ✝ Those who hunger and thirst for righteousness will be filled; their memory a blessing

---

[7] 1 Peter 3:21, Matthew 3:11;6:11;17:5;28:19, Hebrews 2:11, Acts 2:38;19:4, John 3:5;6:35-8, Romans 6:3-4, 1 Corinthians 10:2;12:13, Galatians 3:27, Colossians 2:12, Genesis 3:19, Deuteronomy 8:3, Luke 22:19, Jude 1:5

- ✝ Those who delight and meditate in Yahweh's law
- ✝ Yahweh's waiting servants who will get food, water, health, and fertility
- ✝ Those G-d corrects
- ✝ Full-tithers, who will experience a downpour of heavenly blessings
- ✝ Givers over receivers
- ✝ The mournful, who will be comforted
- ✝ The meek, who will inherit the earth
- ✝ The merciful, who will receive mercy
- ✝ Those cursed and persecuted for following Jesus[8]

Branch & Beauty

Jesus is the Tree of Life. Just as Adam and Eve could choose life, so can we, but only through Jesus: the Root of Jesse, the righteous, kingly **branch** of David. "A branch from His roots will bear fruit." "I am going to bring my servant, the branch." Jesus said that He is the Vine and we are the branches. We can only bear fruit 🍒 rooted and abiding in Him. Similarly, true **beauty** is abiding in the Vine. Jesus is G-d's beauty. Human beauty stems from being created in Jesus' image. Rather than outer looks, beauty resides in the heart, mirroring His "gentle and quiet spirit" and by performing good deeds. Nature's beauty is an appreciation of G-d's creativity. All good is rooted in G-d, who gives life, growth, fruit, and all things beautiful.[9]

Burden-bearer, Bought

Jesus took on all heavy guilt and human-borne **burdens** by **buying** our freedom with His blood 💧. He replaced

---

[8] Genesis 12:3, 1 Peter 1:18, Revelation 5:9;19:9, Ephesians 1:3, John 14:15-7;26;20:26, Matthew 5:3-9, Jeremiah 17:7, James 1:12, Psalms 1:2, Exodus 23:25-8, Job 5:17, Micah 3:10, Luke 6:28, Isaiah 30:18

[9] Isaiah 11:1;10, Jeremiah 23:5, Zechariah 3:8, John 15:5, 1 Peter 3:4, Genesis 1:27, 1 Samuel 16:7

certain curses and condemnation with His easy yoke and light burden. Jesus even offers help with His commands; we can pray for strength and rest for our souls. Grace upon grace. The world continues in tribulation, but Jesus says, "Take heart because I have overcome the world." There is no unbearable burden or temptation: G-d will always provide an escape. "The sufferings of the present pale to the glory to come." Paul exclaims that we will be "hard pressed on every side, but not crushed; perplexed, yet not in despair; persecuted, yet not forsaken; struck down, but not destroyed." Don't do it alone, or you will be crushed. "Cast your burden on Yahweh, for He will never let the righteous be moved." In turn, we must help bear each other's burdens to fulfill Jesus' law, rather than merely mimicking Moses' Law by placing burdens on others without lifting a finger. Rescue the load-fallen donkey of your hater! Moses nearly gave up, asking G-d to kill him rather than have him lead burdensome Israel alone. G-d lovingly shared His Spirit with seventy elders to assist Moses. He will assist us. Just ask. "Cast all of your anxieties on Him, because He cares for you."[10]

---

[10] Psalms 55:22, Galatians 6:2, Matthew 11:28-30; 23:1-4, 1 Corinthians 10:13, 1 Peter 5:7, John 16:33, Acts 20:35, Romans 8:18, 2 Corinthians 4:8-9, Exodus 23:5, Numbers 11:14-7

Cloud & Clothing

G-d's presence and glory manifested in a great **cloud** pillar to protect Israel from enemies and the elements and to guide them in the desert. G-d descended as a cloud atop Mount Sinai to teach the Law and share the Ten Commandments. G-d's presence was a cloud over the mercy seat of the Ark. "Then the cloud covered the Tent of Meeting, and the glory of Yahweh filled the Tabernacle." The cloud later filled the First Temple. The Father's bright cloud shone when Jesus was baptized. When Jesus ascended, a cloud received Him and hid Him in His loving Father's warm embrace. Jesus will return "on the clouds of the sky with power and glory." He will raise the first resurrected and those living in Him on a cloud to Himself.

We now have covering, both from the sky and on Earth. We no longer need to be ashamed of our cold, sinful nakedness like Adam and Eve. G-d **clothed** them in garments of skin. We are clothed in Christ after baptism, and gifted G-d's armor to ward off Satan and evil until Jesus comes again. The Holy Spirit "clothes us with the power from on high." Warm Jesus, whose garment is light, allows us to be dressed in the garments of salvation, wrapped in robes of righteousness. Be worthy of the white garments Jesus wants for you by putting on "compassion, kindness, humility, gentleness, and patience." "Fine linen is the righteous deeds of the saints."[11]

Compassion, Comfort & Care

"Praise be to the G-d and Father of our Lord Jesus Christ, the Father of **compassion** and the G-d of all **comfort**, who comforts us in all our troubles, so that we can comfort those in any trouble with the comfort we ourselves receive from G-d." G-d compassionately forgives iniquity, repeatedly restraining His anger and wrath. G-d has compassion on whom He will have compassion, based on His greater plan, not our effort or desire. But G-d is merciful, hearing and comforting the humble and fearful cries of affliction, suffering, and mourning. G-d's rod and staff (think cross!), steadfast love, and life-giving promise all comforted David. Later, Jesus died so G-d could send our eternal Comforter, the Holy Spirit.

Compassion for His fellow humans motivated Jesus' miracles: He taught, fed, cleansed, healed, and resurrected. Jesus **cares** for, and will take care of, us! Cast your anxious burdens on He who knows us intimately, down to the number of hairs on our heads! Share in Jesus' suffering. He will share in your comfort until He wipes every tear: mourning, crying, pain, and death no more.[12]

Cornerstone and Consecration

Jesus is G-d's most precious, costly and tested chief **cornerstone** for Zion's firm foundation: the living "stone the builders rejected." Faith in Jesus and the Word makes

---

[11] Luke 24:49, Exodus 13:21;24:16; 40:34, 1 Kings 8:10-1, Leviticus 16:2, Acts 1:9, Matthew 24:30, 1 Thessalonians 4:17, Isaiah 61:10, Genesis 3:21, Galatians 3:26-7, Colossians 3:12, Psalms 104:2, Revelation 3:4; 19:9, Ephesians 7:11

[12] 2 Corinthians 1:3-7, Exodus 33:19, Psalms 23:4;55:22;78:38;119:50;76, Exodus 3:7, 2 Chronicles 7:13-4, Matthew 5:4;10:30, Isaiah 49:13, Revelation 21:4, John 14:26

us righteous; works are but a stumbling stone. Believers are living stones, added atop the apostles and prophets' foundation, with Jesus the cornerstone, to build up G-d's spiritual dwelling, the Holy Temple. So **consecrate**—dedicate everything and everyone to firm and unfailing Jesus to protect and guide.[13]

Covenants of Curse, Crucifixion & Communion

The first, **old covenant** (OC), began with <u>Noah</u>. G-d promised with His rainbow 🌈 never again to destroy all life on earth.

The OC with <u>Abraham</u> consisted of three stages: 1. The Covenant Between the Parts promised a son, offspring like stars, and Canaan after 400 years of enslavement. 2. The Covenant of Circumcision changed Abram's name to "Abraham"—"father of many nations," promised kings for descendants, declared that G-d would be Abraham and his descendants' G-d forever, and made the promised land an eternal possession. 3. Abraham's faith to sacrifice Isaac blessed Abraham, making his descendants like stars in the sky and sand on the shore, allowing him to take enemies' lands, and blessing all nations through his seed.

G-d confirmed His covenant with Isaac and Jacob, then remembered His covenant, raising <u>Moses</u> to lead during Hebrew slavery. At Mount Sinai ⚡, G-d made a face-to-face covenant with the Israelites: to be His special treasure above all nations, a priestly kingdom, and a holy nation. Moses splattered blood on the Israelites, saying, "Behold the blood of the covenant that Yahweh had made with you in accordance with these words." The OC was the Law, the Ten Commandments, etched on the tablets of the covenant and stored in the ark of the covenant. G-d renewed His covenant with Moses and Joshua twice each. G-d promised Abraham's

---

[13] Isaiah 8:14;28:16, Psalms 118:22, Ephesians 2:19-22, Romans 9:32-3, 1 Peter 2:8, Luke 9:35

royal descendant <u>David</u> a great name, his son building the Temple for G-d's name, and David's house and kingdom enduring forever.

Keeping the OC meant peace and happiness; breaking it, destruction. The OC was a killer, doomed to be repeatedly broken, being based on the **cursed** letter and Law. Thank G-d for the prophesied **new covenant** (NC), written on the hearts of the houses of Israel and Judah, who would know G-d. G-d would forgive iniquity, never remembering sins again. And thank G-d for the Servant, in whom G-d would make a covenant for Israel and a light for the Gentiles.

The NC is superior to the OC. It is based on better promises, with Jesus its mediator and guarantor. Jesus obediently laid down His life, being **crucified**, hung on a cross-shaped tree †. Jesus was born under the cursed law and OC to redeem us by becoming a curse. The law was weakened by flesh, so G-d had to play both sides to fulfill its righteous requirement: "Sending His own Son in the likeness of sinful flesh and for sin, He condemned sin in the flesh." We can now walk in the Spirit, not the flesh. Jesus humbly canceled all sin-debt of the OC, took away shame, and undid original sin. His body, our sins. His wounds, our healing.

Jesus said at His Last Supper, "This cup is the new covenant in my blood, which is poured out for you." Then G-d brought Jesus back from the dead with the eternal blood covenant. The OC of death is obsolete. The NC gives life. Our old selves are lost, crucified with Jesus. We must be crucified to the world 🌍, and vice versa, "cutting" our flesh's passions and desires. ***Communion*** memorializes Jesus' Last Supper: "For as often as you eat this bread and drink this cup, you proclaim the Lord's death until He comes."[14] It is taken at church as a weekly spiritual tune-up.

---

[14] Genesis 9:13-6;15:13-21;17:1-21;22:17-8;26:2-5;28:13-5, Exodus 2:24;19:5-6;24:8, 2 Samuel 7:5-16, Jeremiah 31:31-4, Hebrews 8:6;13;9:15, Luke 22:20, 2 Corinthians 3:6, Romans 8:3-4, 1 Corinthians 11:26, Galatians 5:24;6:14

Creator

G-d's Word, will, and life-giving breath **created** everything in heaven and on earth. The visible and invisible came from the Father, and by Jesus the Firstborn of all creation, as the Holy Spirit hovered over the formless, timeless void. Humans 🦴 exist for our Father and through Jesus. We are the most precious of all other creations. Nothing exists except through G-d, which makes all things good. Even wicked things were created purposefully for G-d's good plan. Jesus, the Ancient of Days, continues preserving proper functions and holding all things together, including all life. Anyone in Christ is a new creation.[15]

---

[15] Genesis 1:1-2;26, Colossians 1:15-7, John 1:1-3, Hebrews 11:3, Isaiah 42:5, Nehemiah 9:6, 1 Corinthians 8:6, 2 Corinthians 5:17, Job 33:4, 1 Timothy 4:4, Daniel 7:9

Death - Destroyer

One man's lust conceived sin, and sin accomplished is **death** ⌐. But "G-d so loved the world, that He gave His only Son, that whoever believes in Him should not perish, but will have eternal life." "I will remove the sin of this land in a single day." Jesus' free gift removed sin—death's sting—with His first coming; this Man brought resurrection of the dead. The righteous find peaceful refuge, falling asleep and resting from labors in their beds until the first resurrection. Satan can still destroy body and soul in hell; Jesus' purpose in His second coming will be to **destroy** both forever—death swallowed up in victory. Believers whose names are in the Book of Life will be spared from second death—burning forever in a fiery lake of brimstone and sulfur, tormented alongside Death, Hades, Satan, his false prophet, and beastly antichrist.[16]

Deliverer with Dominion

A **deliverer** rescues from harm or danger. G-d delivered Israel from bondage, wicked enemies, fear, and famine using temporary deliverers such as Joseph, Moses, and

---

[16] Zechariah 3:9, John 3:16-7, James 1:15, Romans 5:12;17;6:23, 1 Corinthians 15:20;54-6, 1 Thessalonians 4:14, Revelation 14:13;19:20;20:10-5;21:8, Isaiah 57:1-2, Proverbs 14:32, Matthew 10:28

the Judges. Then, the true deliverer came to Zion for those who turned from sin in Jacob. Jesus rescued "us from this present evil age" by giving Himself up. G-d delivered us from the "domain of darkness" and the grave, bringing us to His beloved Son's kingdom. Jesus also rescues "the godly from trials." Only One with **dominion**—sovereign control—can deliver. G-d's is complete. G-d, in turn, granted humans dominion over all else living. When Jesus was raised from the dead, death 💀 lost dominion over Him. In Jesus' grace, sin lost dominion over us. In return, He asks for dominion over all aspects of our lives![17]

Discipleship: Door to His Dwelling

Jesus' **disciples** must hold His teaching, deny themselves, take up their daily crosses, give up everything and follow Him, and be known for loving each other as Jesus loves them. Neither relationships nor life can block being discipled to the Father's loving will. The Great Commission is to make disciples of all nations. Then the end will come. G-d's **dwelling** is always open to disciples. A disciple must labor hard for G-d's harvest.

G-d "*dead-bolted*" **doors** 🚪 in the Old Testament (OT) to protect the ark from the flood and Hebrew homes from the tenth plague. Jesus is "the Door of the sheep"—a two-way door. Jesus is near, right at our heart's door, listening for our faith knocks. He wants us to enter His protection and salvation. He also knocks for us to let Him in to share a meal—to know us. But, as G-d told Cain, "Sin is crouching at the door." G-d, the judge, waits there too. We must keep our lamps lit, cautious of whom we let in, for Jesus' return. He holds the narrow gate or door of faith open with His Word—get in!

---

[17] Exodus 20:2, Psalms 18:17;30:3;34:4;82:4, Job 5:20, Isaiah 59:20, Galatians 1:4, Colossians 1:13, 2 Peter 2:9, Genesis 1:26;28, Romans 6:9;14

David only asked to spend all his days dwelling in Yahweh's house. So, pray to be "just another brick in the wall"—living stones building up G-d's spiritual dwelling, the holy temple, atop the foundation of the apostles and prophets, Jesus the cornerstone. G-d's Spirit inhabits believers' bodies; Jesus dwells in hearts faithful to His Word. G-d Himself will dwell with His people post-second coming.[18]

---

[18] Genesis 4:7;7:16, Exodus 12:23, John 8:31;13:34-5;10:7;9, Matthew 7:7;13-4;9;38;24:33;25.10,28.19, Revelation 3:7 8;20;21:3, Isaiah 22:22, James 5:9, Luke 9:23;14:26-7;33;13:24-7, Psalms 27:4, Ephesians 2:19-22;3:16, 1 Corinthians 3:16, Colossians 3:16, Proverbs 3:11-2, Acts 14:27

Endure...'til the End

Jesus is the ultimate **endurer**, perfect and sinless through every human test. Suffering and trials—but momentary troubles—are glory and pure joys, producing perseverance, character, then hope until a mature, complete faith lacks nothing. G-d gives an escape from every temptation. But we cannot endure G-d's indignation. Never grow weary, discouraged, or afraid of doing good—the harvest will come. Thank G-d! Like Job, be lovingly steadfast in the Father's will and discipline in order to receive His promised blessings: His kingdom, eternal glory, and crown of life. Keep running G-d's race 🏁 with His encouragement for His prize 🏆! Jesus says, "And behold, I am with you always, to the very **end** of the age." Jesus' return will make Him "the end" after the gospel is proclaimed to all nations. It's near! Until then, patiently endure for your fellow elect saints, hated for Jesus' namesake. Immovably stand in confident faith, hopeful prayer, and the Scriptures. The end is the soul's salvation.[19]

---

[19] Hebrews 3:6;4.15,10.36,12.1;7, Galatians 6:9; Romans 5:3-4;8:25;15:4;5, Deuteronomy 31:8; 2 Corinthians 4:16-8; James 1:2-4;12;5:11;13, Matthew 10:22;24:13-4;28:20, 2 Timothy 2:10, Jeremiah 10:10, Revelation 3:10;14:12, Colossians 1:11-2, 1 Corinthians 15:58;16:13, 1 Peter 4:7-9

Everlasting & Eternal Establisher

G-d has no beginning or end; He inhabits eternity. "I have loved you with an **everlasting** love; therefore, I have drawn you [in] with lovingkindness." The "King **Eternal**" is G-d, whose eternal blood covenant with Jesus' blood raised Him from the dead. G-d "set eternity in the human heart," promising the gift of eternal life before the ages began. Jesus' eternal kingdom awaits! "The way everlasting" is knowing and believing in Jesus and G-d, obeying their words, taking Jesus' living water (blood) and food (body), and sowing to please the Spirit. But one who hates a brother or sister is a murderer, without eternal life.

G-d has set up everything on a firm and permanent basis. G-d **established** creation and our ideals: peace, love, faith, grace, and justice. He enacted His covenants, laws, and churches in faith. G-d established David's kingly throne forever with Jesus. Most importantly, G-d establishes us in Christ. Our Establisher is personal—installing the ways of our steps 👣. *Easter* commemorates G-d's established plan before time: Jesus' resurrection from death on the third day. He is eternal: stone rolled away, empty tomb. "He is not here; He has risen!"[20]

Exalted Eagle

G-d is lifted on high, **exalted** among the nations and on the earth. He is "head above all"—including anything else we idolize. In the ascension, G-d raised Jesus back to the highest place above the heavens, exalting His name above all names. From G-d's right hand, Jesus poured out the Holy Spirit. We must be humble so G-d will lift us up; or the exalted will be humbled. Always focus on the above.

---

[20] Luke 1:30-3;24:2-7, 2 Corinthians 1:21, Jeremiah 10:10;31:3;32:40, 1 Timothy 1:17, John 3:36;4:14;5:24;6:27;54;68;10:28, 2 Peter 1:11, Titus 1:2, Romans 6:23, 2 Thessalonians 2:16; Isaiah 45:18;57:15, Galatians 6:8, 1 John 3:15, 2 Samuel 7:13, Hebrews 8:6;13:9, Acts 16:5

From the Song of Moses: "Like an **eagle** that stirs its nest, that hovers over its young, He spread His wings and caught them, He carried them on his pinions." At Mount Sinai: "You yourselves have seen what I did in Egypt. And how I carried you on eagle's wings and brought you to myself." Wait for Yahweh. Our Father will always catch and bring us close. He gives renewed strength as if soaring on eagle's wings. We will never grow weary or faint. We are safe.[21]

---

[21] Psalms 46:10;57:5;91:4, 1 Chronicles 29:11, Exodus 19:4, Isaiah 40:31;57:15, Acts 2:33, Philippians 2:9-10, Matthew 23:12

Faith...in the Faithful

G-d is **faithful**. He never allows temptations beyond ability and always provides escapes to endure. Jesus was tempted every humanly way and is the founder and perfecter of the most holy **faith**—the "assurance of things hoped for, the conviction of things not seen." Faith is believing the gospel message, Jesus' word, and name; it rests on G-d's power, not man's wisdom. Loving faith in action prepares hearts 🫀 as proper dwellings for Jesus; justifies; reveals G-d's righteousness; pleases G-d, allowing us to see His glory; and is salvation to professing mouths 👄. G-d assigns measures of faith, but may we have Abraham's: at sacrificing Isaac, he trusted his faithful G-d would even raise Isaac. Fight faith's good fight. Always ask in prayer— "Everything is possible for one who believes." Faith's ends are a soul's salvation by grace after baptism, victory over the world, and becoming G-d's child. Faith is a shield against the devil. It heals and never shames. Welcome the weak in faith, not quarreling over opinions. But remember, anything not proceeding from faith is sin.[22]

---

[22] Romans 1:17;10:10-1;14:1;23;12:2-3, Ephesians 2:8;3:16-7;6:16, Hebrews 11:1;6, 2 Corinthians 5:7, Mark 9:23; James 1:3;2:17, 1 Peter 1:9, 1 John 5:4, Galatians 3:26; 1 Timothy 6:12, Jude 1:20, Mark 10:52;11:24;16:16, 1 Corinthians 2:5;10:13, John 1:12;11:40

Fear the Fire; Seek the Fountain

G-d's adopted children in the Holy Spirit live without **fear** or anxiety of bad news, threats, evil, or enslaving death. G-d says, "I am with you," "You are mine." Seek and fear G-d, keeping His commands—the beginning of wisdom and the "whole duty of man." One who suffers for what is right is blessed with G-d's compassion, love, help, protection, and peace. Perfect trusting love casts out fear of punishment, the world, or man—the latter being a trap. Only be afraid of the devil, who can still destroy souls in hell. Turn from evil.

G-dless **fire** is scary. Sodom, Gomorrah, and Korah were a taste of the burning fire and sulfur lake in hell. G-d's wrath will consume disobedient rebels in a second death. In G-d is a good fire 🔥: like a *flashlight* so nothing can hide in darkness, but also guiding and warming our ways. G-d manifested as fire at pivotal Bible junctures: the firepot and torch with Abraham, the un-burning bush introduction to Moses, the desert fire pillar, Mt. Sinai's smoke, fire chariots with Elijah, and the Holy Spirit's Pentecostal introduction. Jesus baptizes in the Holy Spirit with an unquenchable fire to test a heart's faith, refine and purify works, and burn life's chaff—the wicked, worthless parts. Jesus is the extinguisher 🧯 of G-d's fiery anger that we deserve.

Fear of Yahweh, wise teaching, and righteous mouths are **"fountains** ⛲ of life." Jesus is Israel's fountain, opened for David's house and Jerusalem to cleanse all sin and impurity. Fear not when heaven and earth give way. G-d will shorten the great tribulation for the elect's sake. Jesus will then come in blazing fire to guide the survivors to living water springs, welling up to eternal life.[23]

---

[23] Psalms 23:4;34:4;46:2;56:3;68:26;89:46;103:13;111:10;112:7, Isaiah 41:10;13;43:1, Philippians 4:6-7, 1 John 4:18, 1 Peter 3:14, Proverbs 10:11;13:14;14:27;16:6;22;17:3;29:25, Romans 8:15, Matthew 3:12;10:28;24:22, Ecclesiastes 12:13, Hebrews 2:4-5;12:29, Zechariah 13:1, Joel 3:18, John 4:13-4, Revelation 7:17;21:8, Genesis 15:17;19:24, Exodus 3:2;19:18;40:38, 2 Thessalonians 1:7, Luke 3:16, Acts 2:3, Numbers 16:35, 2 Kings 2:11

First: Begotten Born Son & Fruits

Jesus is G-d's **firstborn** creation in G-d's invisible image. G-d pre-chose all believers to be in Jesus' image; He is our firstborn brother, though He later miraculously materialized incarnate as G-d's beloved **first and only begotten Son.** "For to us, a child is born, to us a Son is given." Jesus is also the firstborn of the dead, initiating human life after death 🪦. Now, we can follow!

The law-based OC bore only **fruit** for death; the NC allows good branches to bear good, peaceful, and righteous fruits by abiding in and repenting to Jesus. Jesus' believers are G-d's good fruit harvest for His kingdom. The Great Commission is sharing the gospel to make disciples, more fruit for the kingdom: "The fruit of the righteous is a tree of life, and whoever captures souls is wise." When Jesus returns, He will harvest His "asleep" **firstfruits**, then the living. We must honor G-d with our labor's "firstfruits" and personally develop in the Spirit's fruits and good works. Meanwhile, unproductive 🪴 trees and bad, diseased ones with bad fruits, like false prophets, will be chopped down and thrown into the fire.[24]

The Father's Forgiveness

Forgiveness is not counting a sinner's sins. Right before Jesus committed His Spirit to His **Father**, He said, "Father, forgive them, for they know not what they do." Jesus instantly forgave us, as He taught: not seven times, but seventy-seven. G-d forgives wickedness through Jesus' blood and name. Crimson, scarlet sins are wiped, blotted out, white as snow ❄ or wool 🐑 for final judgment; remembered no more. The forgiving are forgiven by Yahweh, our Father

---

[24] Matthew 3:8;10:7;16 20;9;13:51;17:5;19:30, Acts 26:23, 1 Thessalonians 4:16-7, Proverbs 3:9;11:30, Zechariah 12:10, Exodus 13:1-2, Romans 8:29, Colossians 1:10;15;18, Luke 1:35, Isaiah 9:6, Galatians 5:22-3, John 15:1-7, Philippians 1:11, James 3:18

of Lights: "Forgive us our debts, as we also have forgiven our debtors." Gently, privately rebuke sinners, but forgive believers with each confession and repentance.[25]

Fortress & Foundation

G-d—"Rock and **Fortress** 🏰"—protects the helpless from harm. When Israel only trusted physical strongholds or temples, not learning from Babel or Jericho, G-d made them ruins. But G-d's home, the spiritual temple Zion, will stand firm after heaven and earth. On judgment day, fire will test the quality of believers' work, living stones atop Jesus' perfect, firm **foundation**, sealed with an inscription: "The Lord knows those who are His."[26]

Friend

Jesus is the perfect, unconditional **friend**. Without gossip or separation, He only draws us near: "Greater love has no one than this, that someone lay down His life for His friends." "A friend loves at all times." Jesus loved us with His last breath, asking that our foolishness be forgiven vs. repeating or throwing our offenses back in our faces. Martha and Mary's time with Jesus shows He just wants to spend time with His friends. Martha was so wrapped up in preparing for His visit that she scolded Mary for just wanting to sit with Him. Martha expected Jesus to take her side, but Jesus said Mary had "chosen the good part, which should not be taken away from her." Relationships with G-d, Jesus, and the Holy Spirit are "fellowships."

---

[25] Jeremiah 31:34, Luke 6:37;17:3-4;23:34;46, Matthew 6:12;14-5;18:21-2;26:28, Ephesians 4:32, Isaiah 1:18;43:25;64:8, Acts 3:19;10:43, 1 John 1:9, Colossians 3:12-3, Galatians 6:1, James 1:17

[26] 1 Corinthians 3:11-5, Psalms 18:2;46:1-3, Isaiah 25:2;4, 2 Timothy 2:19, Ephesians 2:20

"The pleasantness of a friend springs from their heartfelt advice," while "wounds from a friend can be trusted." If G-d, Jesus, or the Holy Spirit rebukes us, it can hurt. Humbly take it, knowing that what's best for the flesh is not for the soul. Jesus' friends do what He commands. We are friends, not servants, because Jesus shared His Master's—G-d's—business with us, including knowing that a friend of the world is G-d's enemy. Be like Abraham, a "friend of G-d," who believed G-d, and it was counted to him as righteousness. Walk with the wise to become wise: iron sharpens iron. But "bad company corrupts good character." Companions of "fools" or "unreliable friends soon come to ruin." Bad habits, like befriending "a hot tempered 🌡 " or wrathful person, are addictive.[27]

---

[27] Proverbs 13:20;16:28;17:9;17;18:24;22:24-5;27:6;9;17, John 15:12-5, 1 John 1:3, 1 Corinthians 15:33, James 2:23;4:4, Luke 10:38-42

Gentle, Gracious & Generous

G-d shares His **gentleness, graciousness,** and **generosity** with us to pay forward. Live in abundance. Do not be quarrelsome, slanderous, harsh, violent, cruel, stingy, or mean.

G-d speaks to us in gentle whispers. Jesus describes Himself once: "For I am gentle and humble in heart." Gentleness is a fruit of the Spirit, gained from heavenly wisdom. Unfading inner beauty, a "gentle and quiet spirit," like Jesus, is very precious in G-d's sight. "Make your gentleness evident to all. The Lord [Jesus] is near." A meek spirit is loving, kind, peaceable, courteous, considerate, humble, and patient. But mirroring the Trinity's gentleness does not mean rolling over. We can gently correct our opponents or restore those who sin. Only the strong are gentle, choosing to care for others over being forceful. "A gentle tongue can break a bone" and is a "tree of life." We must also stand ready to gently give testimonies.

G-d's graciousness—with mercy and compassion, "slow to anger and abounding in love"—was taken to the max in the New Testament (NT). It is a saving grace. "He who did not spare His own Son, but gave Him up for us all," how will He not "graciously give us all things"? "For by grace you have been saved through faith." Don't boast; it is not by works. G-d's personalized divine gift of life—grace through Jesus' redemption—was given to us stewards before time.

Grow humbly in Jesus' blessed and sufficient grace, which replaced the law and trains us to renounce ungodliness and worldly passions. "Gracious words are a honeycomb 🍯, sweet to the soul and healing to the bones." Always have gracious speech, "as though seasoned with salt."

G-d generously gives all things, including wisdom. So be ready to share cheerfully and give secretly and quietly. "It is more blessed to give than to receive." "Whoever is generous to the poor [and weak] lends to Yahweh," who will repay. Reap what you sow. Be hospitable to strangers; some, like Abraham, have hosted angels unawares. Test G-d with generosity for overflowing heavenly blessings. Jesus was rich but made Himself poor so we can be rich. Contribute out of poverty, not abundance. Worldly riches are a temptation trap.[28]

Glory to G-d, the Gardener

Our Father **gardener**: You told the earth to sprout vegetation in creation. We lost your beautiful garden. You gave us a second chance in your Son. Adam was a man from dusty earth; Jesus, a Man from heaven. You, **G-d**, are preparing our return to your paradise, the garden in Eden. And this time, the Tree of Life in Jesus will be the only choice, with its healing leaves and monthly fruit; life planted in Jesus' living, unfailing water; harmony with You again; filled with the fruit of righteousness in Jesus; languishing no more. Until then, You will cut off branches in Jesus the Vine that are not bearing disciple-fruit. The gospel seeds must be spread! We can plant and water, but only You, G-d, can grow. You prune us fruit-bearing branches to be more

---

[28] Psalms 18:35;86:15, 1 Peter 3:4;15;4:10;5:10, Galatians 5:23;6:1, Philippians 4:5, Matthew 6:3-4;11:29, Titus 2:11-2;3:2, 1 Timothy 3:3;6:9;18, 1 Corinthians 4:21, Ephesians 1:6;2:4-5;8-9;4:2;7, Proverbs 15:1;4;11:17;16:24;19:17;25:15, 1 Kings 19:12, 2 Timothy 1:9;2:25, Acts 20:35, James 1:5;3:13;4:6, Colossians 4:6, Joel 2:13, Romans 3:24;6:14;8:32, 2 Peter 3:18, 2 Corinthians 8:9;9:6-7;12:9, Hebrews 13:2;16, Malachi 3:10, Luke 21:1-4

fruitful. We must keep repenting to your loving discipline to bear your Spirit's fruits in good works.

"By this my Father is **glorified**, that you bear much fruit and so prove to be my disciples." G-d's presence and name are our glory, more precious than the rarest *gem*. Glory is "Kavod" in Hebrew: weightiness. G-d: Your glory descended on Mt. Sinai ▲, passed by Moses, and filled the tabernacle and temple. Jesus is the radiance of your glory, the exact imprint of your nature. You gave your glory to Jesus before creation. Jesus' face showed it to the world, shared though we all sin and fall short of it alone. Your glory is in all creation and raised Jesus from the dead. Believers with welcome hearts are being transformed from one degree of glory to another, into the spiritual image of Jesus. We give You glory in all bodily actions—even eating and drinking—because we were bought for a price. We are ever thankful. After Jesus' return, there will be no sun or moon: G-d, your glory will be the Light. The Lamb, the Lamp. We glorify You to be glorified, as Jesus always does and is.[29] Amen!

The Good Gift of the Gospel

Extra, extra! Read all about it 📰! The **gospel** is the **good** news! The Word and Way of truth firmly held by its witnesses, then proclaimed through all creation, will bring G-d's glorious end. Of first importance, repent, be baptized, and believe the gospel: that G-d's profound power lovingly ransomed sinless Jesus for all humanity, while we were still sinners. G-d didn't spare His only beloved Son. What else would He withhold? Nothing. Death and condemnation are the wages of sins, but G-d's grace gave the free and

---

[29] Genesis 1:11, Ezekiel 28:13, Isaiah 51:3;58:11, 1 Corinthians 3:7;6:20;10:31;15:47, John 1:14;13:32;15:5;8;17:4-5;24, Hebrews 1:3;12:6, Revelation 2:7;21:23;22:1-2, Jeremiah 31:12, Mark 4:15, Colossians 1:10, Matthew 3:8, Philippians 1:11;2:6-8, Ephesians 5:11, 2 Corinthians 3:18;4:4;6, Romans 3:23, Exodus 24:17;33:18-23;40:34, Psalms 50:23;115:1

freeing gift of undeserved righteousness in being justified through faith, like Abraham, through whom all nations were indeed blessed. Fear G-d and give Him glory. G-d will judge the secrets of men through Jesus. Amen!

The gospel is the light of Jesus' glory. Jesus made Himself a lowly and poor humbled servant. Ever obedient to His Father, to the point of death, Jesus died to peg our sins to His cross, canceling our debt and abolishing death. He was buried and raised on the third day. Salvation is given to those who confess Jesus is Lord, call on His name, believe in Him and His resurrection, and obey His commands—sealed with the promised Holy Spirit to be kingdom heirs and immortal children of G-d. Amen!

G-d's greatest **gift** 🎁 is the gospel: saving grace, the Holy Spirit, and the living water of eternal life. It is the best we can share with others, done simply and heartfeltly, not with eloquent words of wisdom. Otherwise Jesus' cross is emptied of its power. G-d's irrevocable gifts of grace are apportioned by Jesus: prophecy, service, teaching, exhortation, contribution, leadership, mercy acts, wisdom/ knowledge messages, faith/encouragement, healing/miracles by the laying of hands, distinguishing between spirits, and speaking/ interpreting tongues. All good and perfect gifts are from above. And Amen!

The gospel perfectly displays G-d's **goodness,** which is forever loving, merciful, truthful, and upright. Jesus, our "Good Shepherd," humbly said, "No one is good except G-d alone." "Everything G-d created is good." Nothing should be rejected, but received thankfully. G-d's goodness is a fruit of His Spirit, fills the earth, makes His sun rise on evil and good, and sends rain on the just and unjust. But good will overcome evil in the end. No good is withheld from the righteous, those who fearfully wait for G-d. Good works done publicly mirror G-d's goodness, glorifying Him, particularly for the family of believers. Ask G-d to show the "ancient paths," "the good way."[30]

Guide

G-d's cloud and fire **guided** Israel to Canaan, directing and protecting them from the elements and enemies. G-d's Word and counsel straighten, level, and illuminate paths to everlasting glory and peace. Beyond physical direction, we humbly need guidance to live life G-d's way. The Holy Spirit guides in truth, telling of things to come.[31]

---

[30] Acts 2:38;20:24, Colossians 2:13-5, Romans 1:12;16;2:16;5:8;6:23;8:28;10:9;11:29;12:6-8;21, John 3:16-7;36;4:10, 1 Corinthians 12:7-10;15:1-4, Galatians 3:8-9;5:22;6:10, Mark 1:15;10:18;45;16:15-6;24:14, Ephesians 1:13-4;2:8-9;4:7, Revelation 14:7, 1 John 4:9-10, Luke 11:13;24:45-9, 2 Corinthians 5:21, 2 Timothy 1:6;10, Isaiah 52:7, James 1:17, 1 Chronicles 16:34, Psalms 25:8;31:19;33:5, Exodus 34:6, Lamentations 3:25, Matthew 4:45;5:16, 1 Timothy 4:4, Jeremiah 6:16

[31] Proverbs 3:6, Psalms 25:9;73:24;119:105;139:24;143:10, John 16:13, Isaiah 42:16, Exodus 13:21, Luke 1:79

ℋ ✓ h

Helper & Healer

G-d said after making Adam, "It is not good for man to be alone. I will make a **helper** suitable for him." Eve was necessary for Adam. "Unhappy is the man who is by himself, because he has no helper." But Eve was far from perfect, and human interaction requires discernment. Jesus is our perfect helper who during our weakness sent a permanent helper in the Holy Spirit. There is no need to have troubled or fearful hearts because Jesus left His unworldly peace with us. With G-d as the helper of the helpless, fatherless, and widows, "what can mere mortals do?" And, like all of G-d's gifts, help is to be shared. Open your hearts to those in need.

Healer, Yahweh. Most pleas for help are corporeal, the cry of our deteriorating soul casings, our bones in agony, sickbed-ridden, blind, weary, grieved, wounded, brokenhearted. But body is least, less than mind and soul. Faith and G-d's Word restore from Sheol to life. By Jesus' wounds, sickness from sin has been taken away. Speak graciously, confess sins, and pray together to heal fellow believers.[32]

---

[32] Genesis 2:18, Hebrews 13:6, John 14:16;26-7, Psalms 6:2;10:14;30:2-3;31:19;41:3;4;68:5;107:20;146:8;147:3, Romans 8:26, 1 Peter 2:24, Proverbs 16:24;17:22, James 5:16, Exodus 15:26;23:25, Matthew 11:28, Isaiah 40:29

Highest & Holiest

G-d Most **High**—El Elyon—our Tippity Top Apex. You, your ways, and your thoughts are higher. Your Son is our High Priest at your right hand above the heavens ✦ in the "high and **holy** place." Holy, Holy, Holy Father, Son, and Spirit. Sacred and separate, your very names are holy. Jesus, You are the Son of the Highest. The angel told Mary that the "power of the Most High would overshadow" her, and the "Holy One" she birthed would be the Son of G-d. "Israel," G-d's holy nation, is set apart above all nations to fulfill His promise with Jesus through the holy prophets and Scriptures. G-d said "Israel" "will be holy, because I am holy." Your believers, as your temple, have your holy calling: "If the root is holy so are the branches."[33]

Hope ... in Hosanna the Heir

Hope was scarce before Jesus. Original sin left lasting futility: "until you return to the ground, since from it you were taken; for dust you are, and to dust you will return." "Hopes of the wicked come to nothing." The OT's main moral as summarized by Ecclesiastes: one's own strength or merit would always end in being wicked. It was hopeless but for the "G-d of hope's" faithful Word.

The OT, written to instruct and encourage, hinted at a new hope (not Star Wars!). If G-d is our hope, He will renew our strength. G-d knows the plans He has—to prosper, not to harm; to give a future and a hope. Gaining G-d's wisdom makes an unbreakable hope.

"Hope deferred makes the heart sick, but a longing fulfilled is a tree of life." The latter was Jesus, by the power of the Holy Spirit. On Palm 🌴 Sunday, the people cheered, "**Hosannah**, the Son of David. Hosannah in the Highest."

---

[33] Isaiah 57:15, Deuteronomy 28:1, Luke 1:35, Psalms 9:2;40:4, Acts 2:33, Leviticus 11:45, 1 Corinthians 3:17, 2 Timothy 1:9;2:21;3:15, Luke 1:70

Hosannah is a Hebrew plea, "Pray, save us!" Finally hope. Rejoice in a new birth, emboldened in the living, blessed, and purifying hope of Jesus' resurrection until His revelation: eternal life and a glorious inheritance. The call to give testimonies is our patient "reason of hope" of the gospel, to be shared and defended gently and respectfully: hope in Jesus, in His promises, Word, and unfailing love. Lay up your hope in heaven.

G-d's appointed "**heir** of all things" is returning. We can join as fellow kingdom heirs in the gospel's happy ending. Be childlike, meek, humbly poor to the world and in spirit, persecuted, righteous, and rich in faith. Only a child of G-d, born again and justified by Jesus' grace, deserves His grand inheritance as Abraham's "heir of promise." That is what "Israel" means. The Holy Spirit bears witness to and guarantees this heritage. Faith overcoming tribulations, not lineage, makes heirs. Suffer in Jesus to be glorified with Him.[34]

House & Home ... in our Hearts

"But as for me and my **house** 🏠, we will serve Yahweh." This world and earthly dwellings are not our **home**. Shelter is important, but it pales in comparison with our eternal heavenly home. "In my Father's house are many rooms ... I go and prepare a place for you." The church is called to add to G-d's house and Third Temple, built on a sturdy foundation with Jesus as its cornerstone, with our good works until our homecoming to G-d's "holy habitation." Blessed are those with highways to Zion in their **hearts** 💝. G-d loves lovers of Jesus and His teachings, and they both will make a home within our hearts. A person after G-d's

---

[34] Genesis 3:19, Jeremiah 29:11, Romans 8:17;24-5;12:12;15:4;13, 1 Peter 1:3;13;3:15, Matthew 5.3;5;10;21:9, Isaiah 40:31, Ephesians 1:18;2:12, 2 Corinthians 3:12, Proverbs 10:28;13:12;24:14, Psalms 33:18;37:11;118:25;130:5, Titus 1:1;2:13;3:7, 1 John 3:3, Colossians 1:5;23, Hebrews 1:2;11:7, Galatians 3:29, Revelation 21:7, James 2:5, Mark 10:14; John 3:3

own heart, like David, is a little Eden. Closer than ever, we are sojourners until the full glorious Eden returns.[35]

Humble Hero & Horn

Humility, the fear of G-d, opposes pride. G-d sent Jesus as a humble human to serve us, then to die for us. Jesus is perfectly all-powerful, without reason to be humble. Yet He is humble in order to teach that we absolutely must be. Put others first! "G-d opposes the proud, but shows favor to the humble." "For everyone who exalts himself will be humbled" and vice versa. Pride and arrogance bring disgrace, lowliness, and downfall. Humility brings wisdom, victory, riches, life, elevated honor, and salvation. This is the way of evil vs. G-d's way. Jesus called Himself "gentle and humble in heart." Jesus—our perfect, humble **hero!** and a noble Man with outstanding traits: humility, selflessness, courage, genuine goodness—a change-galvanizer. In *hockey* terms, Jesus is our captain, who took a career-ending hit to make the pass for the game-winning goal. We are now Stanley Cup champions for all time. Somehow, He also makes all the saves and permanently removed the penalty box aka the "sin bin."

Ram's **horns** 🐏 trumpet 📯 in celebration, victory, anointed exaltation, and ultimately, salvation. The "horn" symbolizes the reason we lift our heads high: for G-d's glory and name, or our own. Isaac's sacrificial replacement was a ram with entangled horns. The golden sin altar was adorned with horns atop. Jesus became the "horn of salvation," a strong King who sprouted from the House of Israel. G-ds' trumpet will usher in the end of days and Jesus' reign, when the horns of the wicked will be cut off.[36]

---

[35] Acts 13:22, John 14:23, Psalms 39:12;68:5;84:5, Isaiah 28:16, Joshua 24:15, 2 Corinthians 5:1, John 14:2, 1 Corinthians 6:19, 1 Timothy 3:15

[36] Psalms 3:3;18:2;75:10;149:4, James 4:6;10, Luke 1:69;14:11, Proverbs 8:13;11:2;18:2;12;22:4, Matthew 11:29, Mark 10:45, Philippians 2:8, Ezekiel 29:21, 1 Samuel 2:1

Husband and Head

"**Husbands**, love your wives, as Christ loved the church and gave Himself up for her." G-d appointed Jesus' betrothed church: apostles, prophets, teachers, then miracles, gifts of healing, administrating, and various tongues. People come first. Husbands and wives must mutually submit under Jesus. An unbelieving husband can be made holy by his wife, and vice versa. Jesus, the **Head** ✊, loves His church like His own body: only to nourish and cherish, never to defile or treat harshly. Marriage's "becoming one flesh" is analogous to fusing with Jesus, allowing Him to dwell inside hearts in one Spirit. G-d is Jesus' Head; Jesus, the husband's; and husband, the wife's.[37]

---

[37] Ephesians 1:22; 5:21-29;31;33, 1 Corinthians 7:14;11:3;12:28, Hebrews 13:4, Colossians 1:18;3:19, 2 Corinthians 11:2

"I am Who I am"

"I am" and "Yahweh" are both rooted in "being." Moses asked what name to give Israel to prove that the G-d of their fathers sent him to deliver them. G-d replied, "I am who I am." "I am has sent me to you." Yahweh and Jesus both said, "I am He." Jesus said, "I and the Father are One," "before Abraham was, I am!," and simply replied "I am" when asked if He was the Messiah, Son of the Blessed One. Jesus described Himself using "I am" seven times: the Bread of Life; the Light of the World; the Door of the sheep 🐑; the Good Shepherd; the resurrection and the life; the way, the truth, and the life; and the true Vine. G-d and Jesus just are![38] Amen!

Iesous: Immanuel & Image of G-d

Iesous is the NT's Greek name given to Jesus. The angel told Mary she would bear a Son and to call Him Iesous, meaning "salvation." Iesous fulfilled G-d's prophecy of a virgin bearing a child named **Immanuel**—"G-d with us" in Hebrew—who would "save" His people from their sins. We call on all of His powerful names: Iesous, Immanuel, Jesus. The very **image** of the invisible G-d—the exact imprint 👆

---

[38] Exodus 3:14, John 6:35;8:12;24;28;58;10:7;11;30;11:25;13:19;14:6;15:1, Isaiah 41:4;43:10;48:12, Deuteronomy 32:39

of G-d's nature. Humans were created in Iesous' image. Believers were predestined to be conformed to Iesous' heavenly image. To imitate and bear G-d's image![39]

Immortal, Invisible & Incorruptible

"Now to the King eternal, **immortal**, **invisible**, the only G-d, be honor and glory forever and ever. Amen." Only Jesus has seen G-d, whom G-d incarnated to abolish death, bringing to light the gospel—life and immortality. In Jesus, souls are immortal; keeping His word and "eating" His bread ✎ makes us children of G-d and of the resurrection. Steel your mind on the unseen: spirit, not flesh. G-d's power and divinity formed the transient physical and eternal invisible. G-d is **incorruptible**, never changing His mind, lying, or taking bribes. Flesh will be incorruptible when Jesus calls us home.[40]

Inheritance

G-d and "Israel" are each other's **inheritance**. G-d's grace promised His inheritance to Abraham, not depending on the Law. "Israel," Jesus' believers, are G-d's children and heritage: heirs rewarded the promised glorious riches of the eternal heavenly inheritance of the saints in light. This is the *icing* on the cake of G-d's love, and they are sealed 💌 by the Holy Spirit guarantee. But succumbing to evil fleshly acts inherits eternal judgment, torment, and punishment.[41]

---

[39] 2 Corinthians 4:4, Genesis 1:27, Colossians 1:15, Hebrews 1:3, Romans 8:29, Matthew 1:23, Isaiah 7:14, Luke 1:31;2:11, 1 Corinthians 15:49

[40] 1 Thessalonians 4:16-7, Romans 1:20;23, 1 Samuel 15:29, 1 Timothy 1:17;6:16, 2 Timothy 1:10;6:16, John 5:37;6:50;8:51;11:26, Luke 20:36, Matthew 25:46, Colossians 1:16, Hebrews 11:3, 1 Corinthians 9:25, 1 Peter 1:23

[41] Galatians 3:18;29, Revelation 21:8, Romans 8:17, Colossians 1:12;3:23, Ephesians 1:14, Deuteronomy 32:9,

Interceder

Jesus always **intercedes** as the priest between our sins and G-d. "No one comes to the Father except through me." The Holy Spirit intervenes for the saints on what to pray for, according to G-d's will, even with groanings 😯💬 too deep for words. Believers intercede with confession and prayer, healing others' sins.[42]

---
[42] 1 Timothy 2:1-6, Isaiah 53:12, Hebrews 7:25;9:15, James 5:16, Romans 8:26-7, John 14:6

Jealous *Judge*...for us & Jerusalem

"I, Yahweh, your G-d, am a **jealous** ☹ G-d." How blessed that G-d wants us! "They stirred Him to jealousy with strange gods; with abominations they provoked Him to anger." The difference between divine and worldly jealousy is everything. Be jealous for G-d and Jesus only. But find worldly and financial contentment for Jesus' sake through "weaknesses, insults, hardships, persecutions, and calamities." A strong, inordinate desire for others' physical property is coveting: quarrels, fights, theft, adultery, and even murder can ensue. Envy is sinful desire for others' intangible blessings, talents, or achievements, and brings "disorder and every vile practice," rotting the bones. Jealousy is insecurity over one's own possession or relationship, for good or bad. If you feel any conceited, selfish ambition, check in with G-d and ask of Him with good desires to enable you to avoid having furious, vengeful, or bitter hearts.

Ungodliness elicits G-d's consuming, smoky jealousy and wrathful, condemning **judgment**. Jesus first came to save the world, not judge it. G-d has entrusted all judgment to Jesus, the righteous judge, whose day to proclaim "justice to the nations" is coming. When we judge, complain, or speak against others, we judge G-d's law.

Yahweh of Hosts said, "I am exceedingly jealous for Jerusalem and Zion." Jerusalem—Hebrew for "peaceful possession" or "awesome completeness"—is the holiest city on earth, where G-d chose to have His holy name rest, yet it is enslaved. The free and new heavenly Jerusalem— faithful "city of the living G-d" and "throne of Yahweh"— will descend after Jesus returns.[43]

Joy & Justification in Jesus

Mary's visiting angel said, "You will conceive in your womb and bear a son, and you will call His name **Jesus**." G-d named Jesus. Thank you, Jesus, for being born, the real Christmas 🎄 blessing! If we ask in your name, we will receive, so that our **joy** may be full.

Joy 😊 is the Holy Spirit's second fruit. Jesus, your joy of salvation is inner, soulful, heavenly cheer which cannot be taken when our spirits are joined with You through the Holy Spirit—an inexpressible, glorious, and great exuberance in knowing G-d and You and your deep loves. Even the angels want to learn more about "the good news of great joy." We always rejoice in You and G-d's words, names, and testimonies! We count trials and suffering as "pure joy," for they test faith to be steadfast. We sow in tears and mourning to reap with shouts, dancing, and songs of gladness when Jesus' glory is revealed. Jesus will one day rejoice over us with loud singing. We enter our Master Yahweh's joy, which is our strength. "Your consolations cheer [our] soul[s]." We delight in our children walking in truth, wisdom, and righteousness. So does the Father in us.

Justification is G-d's predetermined righteousness through faith and works, not lawfulness. Jesus' obedience— "who for the joy that was set before Him, endured the cross"—justifies in His name and by G-d's Spirit. Jesus'

---

[43] John 5:22;12:47, Isaiah 42:1, 2 Corinthians 11:2;5:10;12:10, Hebrews 12:22;13:5, 1 Corinthians 3:3, James 3:14-6;4:11, Proverbs 6:34;14:30, Deuteronomy 4:24;32:16, Exodus 20:5, Galatians 4:25-6;6:4, Zechariah 8:2-3, Philippians 2:3, Jude 1:15, 2 Timothy 4:8, 1 Kings 11:36, Jeremiah 3:17, Revelation 21:2, Matthew 12:18

blood joins us in gifted grace as heirs of eternal life. G-d promised Abraham to bless all nations through his offspring because all can be justified either by or through faith. Reconciled peace with G-d and the incredible treasure safe-kept in jars of clay awaits! But we must be careful with our words; they can justify or condemn.[44]

---

[44] Matthew 1:21;12:37;25:21, 1 Corinthians 6:11, John 15:11;16:22-4, Philippians 4:4, Galatians 3:8;5:22, 1 Peter 1:8;1?;4:13, Romans 3:24-30;5-9;19;8:30;15:13, Nehemiah 8:10, Jeremiah 15:16, Psalms 16:11;30:11;51:12;94:19;119:14;111;126:5 , Zephaniah 3:17, 3 John 1:4, Luke 2:10, James 1:2, Proverbs 23:24, Titus 3:7, Hebrews 12:2

Kadosh

Kadosh is Hebrew for "holy." G-d's majestic splendor is unlike anything. His hallowed name rests in the holiest of holies, Kodesh Ha'Kadoshim. G-d's holy temple ✡ and Spirit reside in us believers until Jesus' second coming! Then the Holy Place will descend. "Holy, Holy, Holy is Yahweh of Hosts; the whole earth is full of His glory." "Holy, Holy, Holy, is the Lord G-d Almighty, who was and is and is to come." G-d's "holy calling" for us in Jesus exists because G-d and Jesus are holy. We are to be ready for every good work, useful to the Master of the house.[45]

Keys of David, Death & Knowledge

Jesus holds the house of **David's key** ⚷ to the kingdom on His shoulder. What He opens cannot be shut, and vice versa. Jesus gave Peter the heavenly kingdom keys, saying, "Whatever you bind [or loose] on earth shall be bound [or loosed] in heaven." Jesus holds the keys of **death** and Hades/Sheol through His resurrection. Jesus rebuked the legalistic Pharisees for blocking themselves and others from Him, the "key of **knowledge**." "Fear of Yahweh is

---

[45] 1 Peter 1:15-6, Isaiah 6:3, 1 Corinthians 3:16-7, Hebrews 12:14, 2 Timothy 1:8-9;2:21, Psalms 24:2;96:9, Revelation 4:8, Matthew 6:9, Job 28:28

the beginning of knowledge," bolstered by guidance, intelligence, discernment, wisdom, and discipline. "The full riches of complete understanding" is knowing G-d's mystery: Jesus and the truth of salvation. Knowing G-d and Jesus is grace and peace, pleasant to the soul. Utterance of knowledge is a spiritual gift. G-d and Jesus most want to know us, and that the earth be filled with the knowledge of their glory.[46]

Kind Keeper

G-d has shown His "everlasting kindness" to humanity, even the ungrateful and wicked, never forsaking us. G-d's lovingkindness motivates us to repent. Jesus' analogy of Him being the true Vine, us the branches, and G-d the vineyard keeper perfectly displays His nurturing kindness. Keep G-d's kindness to remain in it or be cut off. "G-d bless you and **keep** you" from wandering. G-d's greatest kindness is the saving grace of Jesus—"one keeper" from David who guides "Israel." He is the chief, great keeper who "gives His life for the sheep;" then they scattered. He knows us, and we Him. We share G-d's kindness with others, a fruit of the Holy Spirit. Lastly, a strike or rebuke from the righteous is a kindness to get back on track.[47]

King & Kingdom

G-d is the "**King** Eternal" of Glory. "Your kingdom come. Your will be done. On earth, as it is in heaven." Jesus is "King of kings and Lord of lords," called "King of Israel" as He rode into Jerusalem on a colt donkey. He didn't come to conquer: His **kingdom** is not of this world. When Jesus

---

[46] Isaiah 22:22, Revelation 1:18, Luke 1:77;11:52, Proverbs 1:5;7;2:10;12:1;15:14;18:15, 1 Corinthians 12:8, Colossians 2:2, Habakkuk 2:14, John 8:32, Matthew 16:19

[47] 1 Corinthians 13:4, Ephesians 2:7, Romans 2:4;11:22, Psalms 121:5;141:5, Isaiah 54:8, Luke 6:35, Ezekiel 34:23, Matthew 2:6;26:31, John 10:11-4;15:1, Numbers 6:24

returns, the persecuted and righteous family of born-again, childlike, and spiritually poor disciples will be richly welcomed into G-d's heavenly, eternal kingdom—where *kites* cannot fly. It is near. The kingdom is about power, not talk; being righteous, peaceful, and joyous in the Holy Spirit, not eating and drinking. Every knee will bow to Jesus atop David's throne, holding Judah's scepter of uprightness, draped in His blood-dipped purple robe. The last on earth, serving all, will be first in the kingdom.[48]

---

[48] Matthew 3:2;5:2;10;6:9-10;7:21;18:3;19:14, 1 Timothy 1:17, Zechariah 9:9, John 3:3;18:36, 2 Peter 1:11, Revelation 17:14, Psalms 24:10, Romans 14:17, 1 Corinthians 4:20

L 🏮 l

The Lion, the Lamb & the Last

Jesus is paradoxically the Lion and the Lamb, both fiercely atop the food chain and also a gentle slaughter. Jacob's blessing hinted at the **Lion** 🦁 of Judah, which Revelation explicitly calls Jesus. He is King of kings of the jungle earth, boldest and mightiest. But as a man, He didn't show force. He only did what His Father commanded.

Jesus is also the Passover **Lamb** 🐏 of G-d because He so closely identifies with us fellow sheep: leading, but also alongside. His sacrifice made us new and "unleavened" of the old, sinful ways. Lambs are a richly steeped biblical foreshadowing metaphor. G-d provided Abraham a lamb as an offering instead of Isaac; lamb's blood on Hebrew doorposts protected from the death of the firstborn, the tenth plague in Egypt; and a lamb was one of the few animals sacrificed to G-d which atoned for sins. Jesus was the perfect Lamb "slain from the creation of the world," and "led to slaughter." Innocent blood makes the sinful clean. Jesus' is the most precious and will defeat Satan. Revelation mostly refers to Jesus as the Lamb, but He will return the mighty, kingly **Lion**: "Weep no more; behold, the Lion of the tribe of Judah, the Root of David, has conquered, so that He can open the scroll [The Lamb's Book of Life] and its seven seals." Then will come the wedding of the Lamb to His church.

Jesus is with us through the "last hour" until the end, when He will take His power back, and this human experiment comes to a merciful, awesome close. Jesus is the "**last** Adam," fixing his and humanity's error forever. Jesus had His "Last Supper" as a human because He will return fully divine to raise us on the last day.[49]

Lawgiver of Liberty

G-d is the only **Lawgiver** and judge: able to save or destroy. G-d made the law of righteousness known and testified to in the Torah and Prophets Books 📕: that Jesus' believers become righteous. Judah is the "Lawgiver" because Jesus abolished the cursed Law which made sin known and aroused sinful passions unto fearful death. Jesus is the "end of the law," replacing it with His law of the Spirit—truth, grace, life, and **liberty**—fulfilled by G-d's servants bearing each other's burdens. The law ends at death, and we die under the baptizing water. We become free of sin. Against the fruits of the Holy Spirit, there is no law. Moses' law was our guardian before Jesus, and every iota and dot of it will be accomplished before heaven and earth pass away.[50]

Light, Life & Love

"G-d is **light**," dwelling in an unapproachable light. G-d's Word, a marvelous "*lamp* for [our] feet," lights our paths. Jesus came as the "light of the world" and to the Gentiles; once in darkness, we are now in His light. With enlightened

---

[49] Isaiah 53:7, 1 Corinthians 5:7;15:45, Revelation 5:5;12:11;13:8;19:7, Genesis 22:8;49:9, Proverbs 28:1;30:30, John 1:29;6:39, 1 Peter 1:19, Exodus 12:7, 1 John 2:18
[50] Romans 3:20;5:14;6:14-6;7:1-6;8:1-3;10:4, Matthew 5:18;22:36-40, Galatians 3:10;24;5:23;6:2, Revelation 22:3, James 1:25;4:12, Genesis 49:10, Psalms 60:7, John 1:16-7

hearts, shine His light in good deeds. Bring glory to G-d, the Father of lights. May G-d's radiant face shine on the fellowship, the united children of light. Share the gospel, the "message of light." After time, there will be no sun or moon. G-d will be our light, and Jesus our lamp. "Whoever follows me will never walk in darkness, but will have the light of life."

You are **life**, G-d. You breathed your breath of life into our nostrils. You have life in yourself and granted Jesus to have life in Himself too. We live for You through Jesus: "I am ... the life. No one comes to the Father except through me." Please govern our minds by your Spirit, not flesh, so we may live to the full. Keep your life-giving word on our lips always. Guard our lips to preserve our lives. Not our lives, but yours! Our lives reflect our hearts. If our hearts are right, You will guard our lives. We believers are promised the crown of life, and "rivers of living water will flow from within" when we keep Jesus' commands faithfully and stay in His and your love, ever praying in your Spirit. Persecution comes in godliness, but we are willing to lose our lives to find life eternal. Live or die, we are in Jesus. "For G-d so loved the world that He gave His only Son, that whoever believes in Him will not perish but have eternal life." "Whoever lives in love lives in G-d, and G-d in them."

"G-d is **love** 🤘." The greatest love story is a Father's love for His Son whom He sacrificed in His unfailing, abounding love for us. G-d lavished His inseparable love, making us His children. We love because G-d loves us first. Jesus said, "Greater love has no one than this, that someone lay down his life for his friends." The law is fulfilled in the greatest commandments: to fully love G-d, then love one another as oneself. Jesus' new command is to love one another as He loved us, even to death. All things work for good for those who love G-d. Nothing in all creation can separate us from G-d's love in Jesus. Jesus rebukes and disciplines those He loves.

Always walk in sincere, perfect love: it binds all virtues together in perfect harmony. Love is life's top building block: faith → goodness → knowledge → self-control → perseverance → godliness → mutual affection → love. Love is the first fruit of the Spirit: G-d's quieting love poured into our hearts through His Spirit. Love "covers a multitude of sins" and is the greatest when only it, faith, and hope remain. Love builds up, while knowledge puffs up, and it never ends, unlike prophecy, tongues, and knowledge. Love is self-sacrificial, patient, kind, and serves humbly. It is not envious, boastful, arrogant, rude, self-seeking, irritable, or resentful. Love "keeps no records of wrongs;" rejoices in truth, not evil; and "protects, trusts, hopes, and perseveres" in all things. Love all, even enemies and persecutors.

But loving the world is not loving G-d. G-d's love doesn't abide in those who close their hearts to the needy. Faith or boastfully giving sans love is nothing; speech without love, a clanging gong. Loving money is the "root of all kinds of evil," such as wandering from faith.[51]

Lord Leader

Jesus literally washed feet 🦶 as our **Lord**. We must "wash" feet by humbly serving others. With all power and authority, Jesus is still so humble. Faithful and only Sovereign Lord Jesus, You are humble without reason. In the Holy Spirit, our tongues confess that You are Lord of lords, Sabbath, dead, living, and all! Let us know You, call on your name, do G-d's will, and be in your presence as your people.

Hebrew **leaders**—patriarchs, servants, judges, prophets, and kings—were a mixed bag. Some were good with timely qualities; some not. All had their sinful slip-ups. Jesus was,

---

[51] 1 Corinthians 8:1;13:4-8;13;16:14, Romans 5:5;8:6;28;39;12:9;14:8, James 1:12;17, 1 Timothy 6:10;16, 1 John 1:7;3:1;4:16-9, John 3:16;5:26;8:12;10:10;14:6;15:12-3, Psalms 119:105;130, Matthew 5:16;43-8;16:25;22:36-40, 1 Peter 2:9;4:8, Ephesians 1:18;5:8, Acts 13:47, Revelation 21:23, Numbers 6:24, 1 Thessalonians 5:5, Proverbs 13:3;27:19, Genesis 2:7, Colossians 3:14, Zephaniah 3:17, Galatians 5:22

is, and always will be the "baby bear" 🐻 of leaders: just right and what is needed. Jesus came "not to be served but to serve." Leaders should be self-sacrificial, not seeking personal gain, able, G-d-fearing, trustworthy, and bribe haters. Church leaders must also be "above reproach, faithful to [wives], temperate, self-controlled, hospitable, respectable, able to teach, not [a drunkard], not violent ... [or] quarrelsome, not a lover of money," gentle, unconceited, upright, holy, disciplined, sincere, lovers of good, respectful with own family, having obedient children, non-recent converts, of good reputation with outsiders to not be trapped by the devil, with a clear conscience holding the deep truths of faith, not of malicious talk, and tested.[52]

---

[52] 1 Timothy 3:1-13;6:15, Matthew 7:21-3;20:28, Romans 10:9;12-3;14:9, 1 Corinthians 12:3, 2 Thessalonians 3:3, John 13:14, Philippians 2:3, Titus 1:7-9, Exodus 18:21

M m

Majestic & Mighty

"Make known to the children of man your **mighty** deeds, and the glorious splendor of your kingdom." Yahweh reigns, regally robed in **majesty**, splendor, dignity, greatness, and grandeur. His voice, name, and holiness—our awe. G-d's majestic glory called down to Jesus when He was baptized. Jesus now sits at the mighty right hand of His Father, the majesty on high. Lord G-d Almighty's mighty hand will exalt those humbling under it. Depend on His strength and power, not yours. His physical prowess is unrivaled, not to mention His spiritual supremacy. Jesus is all-powerful with His word and through His resurrection. He now holds Judah's mighty scepter. "All authority in heaven and on earth has been given to Me." A righteous person's prayer also has great power. But remember, "not by might nor by power, but by [G-d's] Spirit."[53]

Merciful Maker & Master

G-d, Father of **mercies**, You delight in showing mercy, wanting all sinners to be saved. We deserve your staying angry at us forever, but You are rich in mercy. It renews daily. Only the merciful get your mercy. Your mercy goes

---

[53] Hebrews 8:1-4, Job 37:22, Psalms 8:1;29:4;93:1;104:1;110:2;145:12, Exodus 15:11, 2 Peter 1:17, 1 Peter 5:6, Zechariah 4:6, James 5:16, Matthew 28:18

far beyond withholding wrath or anger, being motivated to help others through active compassion. Your mercy is what will bring eternal life, being made anew in Jesus.

This is all the magnificent handiwork of G-d our **maker**! We are the clay of our potter. You wove us together in our mother's wombs. You know all our knitted parts. We praise You because we are fearfully and wonderfully made. We believers are your workmanship, prepared beforehand to be created in Jesus for good works. Your creations continue well after creation. You keep the world ⊕ spinning, maintaining all life. Every advancement is yours. We cannot wait to see more creations, until your new heaven and earth.

We cannot serve two **masters.** Be a slave to righteousness through obedience to our heavenly, impartial Master maker, G-d; or to worldly sin like monetary greed, and onto death. G-d and Jesus' mercy freed us. We should not waste it to cover up fleshly evil, but by lovingly being a "bondservant of G-d," serving one another. G-d appoints human hierarchies, governments and bosses, directing us to respect authorities to represent G-d well. Whatever work you do, do it wholeheartedly, for G-d, not man. In G-d's hierarchy, the servant or slave is equal in Jesus.[54]

Mediating Messiah of Miracles

Messiah—Mashiach in Hebrew and Christ in Greek—means "Anointed One." ▌ Jesus was set apart, as the promised permanent political and military Leader, Deliverer, Savior, and the NC **Mediator** between humans and G-d. The OC had no godly Mediator and was doomed. When Jesus returns, He will fulfill all after-days prophecy.

---

[54] Ephesians 2:4;10;6:9, Psalm 95:6;139:13-4, Isaiah 64:8, Jeremiah 1:5, Colossians 1:17;3:22-4, Romans 13:1, 1 Peter 1:3;2:13-7, 1 Timothy 6:1, Galatians 5:13, Jude 1:21, Lamentations 3:22-3, 2 Samuel 22:26, Micah 7:18, 2 Corinthians 1:3, Matthew 5:7, 2 Peter 3:9

Miracles and signs are powerful messages to us. Our response should be to give glory to G-d through Jesus—the real *magic*. G-d Himself gave the sign of the virgin giving birth to a Son. Jesus' earthly miracles were all driven by mercy for others. He was moved to pity to stand between humans and the devil's afflictions.[55]

Medicine

"A joyful heart is good **medicine**." G-d is joy and true medicine. You will joyously love yourself—your soul, mind, and body, in that order—if you internalize how much G-d loves you! Take that pill 💊! "For while bodily training is of some value, godliness is of value in every way, as it holds promise for the present life and also for the life to come." Consecrate every day, everything, and everyone to G-d and Jesus. The rest, like health, will take care of itself. Jesus, the true physician, came for the sinners: "It is not the healthy who need a doctor, but the sick." Sickness and death are by-products of the devil's oppressing sin. "Cast your anxieties on [Jesus], because He cares for you." When Jesus returns, the Tree of Life's leaves will heal all nations. Faithful prayer can also restore and heal diseases.[56]

Morning Star

Jesus is the bright **morning star**, fulfilling the prophecy "a star ✡ will come out of Jacob." At Jesus' birth, a new star rose, the brightest shining. We must keep our "lamps" lit, "shining in a dark place, until the day dawns and the morning star rises in [our] hearts." Satan is called Lucifer,

---

[55] 1 Timothy 2:5, Hebrews 9:15, Isaiah 7:14

[56] Matthew 9:12, Proverbs 17:22, Revelation 22:2, James 5:15, 1 Peter 5:7, 1 Timothy 4:8

meaning "brightness," a "day star, son of dawn" to confuse. Don't be fooled: he isn't bright 💡!⁵⁷

Music

Music 🎶 is a vital way of praising G-d and Jesus, "addressing one another in psalms and hymns and spiritual songs, singing and making melody to the Lord with your heart." There are ten Jewish songs of praise:

1. Adam's for Sabbath, either after creation or when G-d forgave original sin
2. Moses and Miriam's after G-d's Red Sea split miracle
3. The Israelites' when G-d gave water in the desert
4. Moses and Joshua's warning right before Moses' death
5. Joshua's after the sun miraculously stood still
6. Deborah and Barak's after G-d delivered Israel from Canaan
7. Hannah's for becoming pregnant with Samuel after hardship
8. David's for his established monarchy. His Psalm musical pieces "sing for joy to Yahweh."
9. Solomon's Song of Songs, a man and woman's love story, allegorically G-d and His people
10. The Coming Messiah's, the Lamb Jesus: in the NT, John the Baptist's father sang for his son being the "prophet of the Most High" who prepared the way for Jesus' salvation. Mary sang for G-d blessing her with Jesus.⁵⁸

---

[57] Matthew 2:2, Numbers 24:17, Revelation 22:16, Isaiah 14:12-3, 2 Peter 1:19
[58] Psalms 18;92, Exodus 14:30-15:19, Numbers 21:16-8, Deuteronomy 32:1-52, Joshua 10:12-5, Judges 4:4-5:31, 1 Samuel 2:1-10, Song of Songs, Revelation 9:9-10, Ephesians 5:19, Luke 1:46-56;67-80

Mystery

G-d's **mystery** ⟨?⟩ revealed is Jesus incarnate, in whom hides all the treasures of wisdom and knowledge. We are blessed stewards of the mystery hidden for ages in G-d for the generations prior. The faith and gospel's mystery of G-d's kingdom has been revealed through the Holy Spirit, and makes the angels jealous: that Jesus came for Jew and Gentile as co-heirs. The mystery from which godliness springs is great: that Jesus "appeared in the flesh, was vindicated by the Spirit, was seen by the angels, was preached among the nations, was believed on in the world, was taken up in glory." Much mystery remains around how resurrected bodies will change, and the "profound mystery" of Jesus and the Church "becoming one flesh." Evil mystery surrounds the man of lawlessness, Satan's son of destruction, who will try to trick believers with "miracles," proclaiming himself "god" and leading a rebellion before Jesus destroys him. All G-d's mystery will be fulfilled when Jesus returns, after seventh trumpet's sound.[59]

---

[59] 1 Timothy 3:16, 2 Thessalonians 2:3-4;7, Matthew 13:11, Ephesians 3:4-9;5:31-2, Romans 16:25, 1 Corinthians 2:7;4:1;15:51, Revelation 10:7

 n

Nail

Biblical **nails** save from destructive oppression. Under Deborah, Israel was saved by a tent peg used to kill her military oppressor. King Solomon wrote, "The words of the wise men are like goads, their collected sayings like firmly embedded nails, given by one shepherd." This embodies Jesus' crucifixion. Our oppressive, sinful debt under the OC was nailed ⚒ to Jesus' cross, through His body. Our relationship with G-d is now fastened: "It will not totter." But heed this warning against false prophets: "Unless I see in His hands the imprint of the nails, and put my finger into the place of the nails, and put my hand into His side, I will not believe." The proof is in the nail. "I have engraved you on the palm of my hands." We deserved the nail but were spared. Feel it piercing through you.[60]

Name

G-d, "Hallowed is your **name**." The Levitical priestly blessing puts Yahweh's name on the receiver. G-d gave Jesus the name above all names, the "name under heaven given among men by which we must be saved": Jesus, Immanuel. Jesus' name glorifies us, and we are justified in It. Calling

---

[60] Isaiah 41:7;49:16, Ecclesiastes 12:11, Judges 4:21, John 20:25, Colossians 2:14

on Jesus' names saves. So bear up for Jesus' namesake. All words and deeds should be "in the name of the Lord Jesus, giving thanks to G-d the Father through Him." We are baptized in the names of the Father, the Son, and the Holy Spirit—the only way to get our names written in the Book 📘 of Life. That is why a good name is better than great riches. Jesus will return with a new name, over which every knee will bow and tongue will confess He is Lord. Jesus' co-conquerors will have G-d's, the new Jerusalem's, and His new names written on them. What beautiful, powerful, and reverent names! We can perform miracles and heal each other with full faith in Jesus' name. What we ask for in Jesus' name, G-d will give. When two or more believers gather in Jesus' name, He is among them. "A threefold cord is not easily broken."[61]

Near & New

G-d and Jesus are **near**. More lovingly, they want to be. G-d is close to the brokenhearted and those who call on Him in truth, taking hold of their right hand. Draw near to G-d, and He will draw near to you. We were once afar, but Jesus' blood has brought us all near. G-d wants all humans to be His elect and possession with no nationality, race, or religion left out. Just answer the call 📱. Without anxiety, seek Jesus, and He will lay His right hand on you. No one can snatch believers from G-d's and Jesus' hands. Actively make your hearts good dwellings, and they will be there! G-d's blessed gift, the Holy Spirit, makes our bodies His temple. Repent and pray before G-d's nearing kingdom comes and all things end.

Being close to G-d and Jesus is contingent on being born again in a **newness** of life: new creations or selves; new hearts of flesh, not stone; and of a new Spirit. The old

---

[61] Ecclesiastes 4:12, Proverbs 22:1, John 15:16, Acts 4:12, Romans 10:13, Matthew 6:9;18:20;28:19, Revelation 3:12, Philippians 2:9-11, Colossian 3:17, James 5:14

is gone. Jesus is "making all things new" until He brings new heavens and earth. G-d, renew our souls, minds, bodies, strength, love, and knowledge in Jesus! Refresh us with Your spiritual *noodle soup*. Your mercies are new every morning 🌄![62]

---

[62] 2 Corinthians 5:17, Philippians 4:4, James 4:8, Matthew 3:2, Psalms 34:18;145:18, Ephesians 2:13, 1 Peter 1:3;4:7, Acts 17:27, 1 Corinthians 6:19, Ezekiel 36:26, Isaiah 40:31;41:13;65:17, Lamentations 3:23, Revelation 21:5, Colossians 3:10, Romans 6:4;12:2, Galatians 6:15

Obedient Offering

Obey G-d, not man. "This is the whole duty of man." G-d shares His Spirit, provides, and fights enemies for His treasured possessions who fully obey and keep His covenant. Jesus lovingly obeyed His Father's will all His life onto death. Adam's disobedience 🍎 made many sinners. Jesus' obedience made many righteous. Jacob blessed Judah's kingly offspring with "obedience of the peoples." Jesus, as eternal salvation's source, asks us to faithfully keep all His commands as His loving friend. Jesus learned obedience in suffering—so must we. We must also obey ruling authorities and parents.

Jesus' ultimate obedience was as the perfect, holy, righteous, permanent, and sinless **offering** to G-d. Willfully sinning while knowing Jesus' truth undoes His sacrifice. G-d wants obedience and love, not animal sacrifice. "The offerings of Judah and Jerusalem will be pleasing to Yahweh" as in the days of old and former years. Jesus' blood and body sacrifice is the only fragrant, sweet aroma pleasant to G-d. Believers are atoned for and sanctified once and for all by Jesus' offering. Our bodies are living sacrifices in spiritual worship.[63]

---

[63] Exodus 19:5;23:22, 2 Corinthians 10:5, Ephesians 5:2;6:1, Hebrews 5:9;10:10;26;13:17, John 14:15;31;15:14, Romans 3:25;5:8;19;12:1;13:1, Acts 5:32, Philippians 2:6-8, Ecclesiastes 12:13

One Opener & Overcomer

"Hear, Israel. Yahweh our G-d. Yahweh is **One**." "One G-d and Father of all, who is over all and through all and in all." Jesus, who is called "G-d," said, "I and the Father [The Holy One of Israel], are One." Three, with G-d's Spirit, as One, exist in perfect harmony. Jesus and His baptized Church become one flesh and body: all one in Jesus. We have one Lord, one Mediator, one faith, one Spirit, one baptism. We are given a variety of gifts, same Spirit; many services, same Jesus; and ample activities, same empowering G-d. Neo has nothing on Jesus: *the One*, the living "One." Jesus unplugged us from the sin matrix. "There is salvation in no one else."

G-d **opens** eyes, hearts, and wombs. The heavens opened at Jesus' baptism and ascension, and they will again when G-d's heavenly kingdom descends in Jesus' reign. Jesus **overcame**, becoming the only one worthy to open the Book of Life's seven seals. "In the world you have tribulation, but take courage; I have overcome the world." If we remain faithful, we receive G-d's heritage as His children:

- † sitting by Jesus on His throne;
- † eating from the Tree of Life in G-d's paradise 📖;
- † authority over all nations;
- † being pillars in G-d's temple;
- † wearing white garments;
- † our names kept in the book of life;
- † hidden manna;
- † white stones engraved with our new names;
- † the names of G-d, the new Jerusalem city, and Jesus' new name written on us;
- † and no hurt from second death.

After tribulation, war, and Satan's final failed coup attempt, good and light will overcome evil and darkness.[64]

Ordained Omega

G-d's power and wisdom confer holy orders on spiritual leaders. Priests and kings were **ordained**, but Jesus was oathfully ordained as permanent High Priest, judge, and King. Jesus ordained His apostles. Believers are witnesses pre-ordained into Jesus' priesthood forever. G-d and His ordained Jesus are the **Omegas Ω**—the last letter of the Greek alphabet—with us through the end times: tribulation, the day of the Lord and judgment, and G-d's holy kingdom come.[65]

---

[64] Isaiah 1:4, John 1:5;10:30;16:33, Ephesians 4:4-6, 1 Corinthians 12:4-6;13, Galatians 3:28, 1 Timothy 2:5, Mark 12:29, Revelation 1:18;2:7;11;17;26;3:5;12;21;21:7
[65] Mark 3:14, John 15:16, Acts 1:22;10:42, Romans 13:1, 1 Corinthians 2:7, Revelation 1:8;22:13

Parable-Preacher

Jesus fulfilled prophecy by using allegorical stories—**parables**—to teach spiritual lessons. But His parables alone miss the mystery of G-d's Kingdom, hidden since the world's foundation. By title and moral:

<u>The Lamp</u>: Shine your light everywhere in good deeds to glorify G-d. Don't hide it, or G-d's gift will be transferred to others.

<u>The Speck & the Log</u> 📖 : Any judgment is hypocritical, so work on yourself first. Then try to heartfeltly help others.

<u>The New Cloth & Old Garment</u>: Moods and actions should match situations, above rituals.

<u>The Divided Kingdom</u>: G-d's kingdom diametrically opposes Satan's work. Neither self-sabotage.

<u>The Sower</u>: Hearing and understanding the word is planting in the good soil of your heart, producing exponential believer-crops. If you only hear the word, the devil snatches, trouble and persecution wither, or life's worries and wealth's deceit choke it out.

<u>The Weeds Among the Wheat</u>: Satan's children are weeds amongst our plants, G-d's children. Let both grow. Angels will harvest the good and burn the bad at the end of the age.

<u>The Mustard Seed</u>: The tiniest seed becomes the largest, most useful tree. A little faith goes a long way.

The Leaven: G-d's kingdom is yeast to flour, raising the dough.

The Hidden Treasure & Pearl: G-d's precious kingdom is worth everything you got!

The Net: G-d will catch all but will basket the good fish and discard the bad.

The Heart of Man: Food comes out, even if eaten with unwashed hands. But words from the mouth come from the heart. Evil thoughts stay and defile.

The Lost Sheep: G-d pursues each of us so we can live. He is happier to have one more repent than ninety-nine remain.

The Unforgiving Servant: We owe G-d infinitely more than others owe us. If G-d is merciful, we must be merciful or we will get what we actually deserve.

Laborers in the Vineyard: G-d's kingdom is believers' negotiated pay. Avoid comparing reward order, time, energy, or work ethic. First will be last, and the last first.

The Two Sons: Be the child who does not wait for G-d's message.

The Tenant Farmers: Religious leaders reject G-d when they reject G-d's prophets and Son—the cornerstone—and will be crushed.

The Wedding Banquet: Don't reject G-d's kingdom invitation. Be clothed in Christ or suffer the same fate as the rejectors.

The Budding Fig Tree: The events leading up to Jesus' second coming have begun. It is near.

The Faithful & Wicked Servant: We don't know when our Master will return. Be faithful. Don't squander His possessions, mistreat your co-servants, or be caught sleeping.

The Ten Virgins: Keep your faith meter full, ready for Jesus' return. There are no second chances.

Ten Talents: "Good and faithful servants" grow G-d's believers. Don't squander G-d's gifts, or they will be given to non-wasters, with you left out in the cold.

Growing Seed: G-d grows His kingdom, even imperceptibly. But the harvest will come at once.

The Good Samaritan: "Neighborly" love is attending even to strangers—not your "kind"—and showing kindness to all.

The Friend at Midnight: Persistently ask for what is right, and G-d will give. He loves our bother.

The Rich Fool: Don't live to accumulate possessions. You can't take them with you. Be rich toward G-d.

The Barren Fig Tree: Don't give up based on your timing. It's all in G-d's time.

The Invited Guests: Be humble, and you'll never be ashamed. But pride precedes the fall. Do kind acts that cannot be repaid.

The Lost Coin 🎰: G-d and His angels rejoice each time a person is found, no matter how many are already saved.

The Prodigal Son: No one is too far from repenting back into G-d's open, gracious arms. Righteous, do not be jealous of "prodigals"—repentant sinners— you already have what the prodigals get.

The Rich Man & Lazarus: Be gracious and generous now. You can't cross from hell to heaven or vice versa after judgment.

The Persistent Widow: Always pray. If an unjust judge eventually gives in to persistent requests, how much faster will our just G-d?

The Pharisee & Tax Collector: Ceremonies don't separate one from sinners. Humbly ask G-d for mercy. We all are sinners.[66]

A *poker* parable: You are "head's up"—mano a mano—in a poker tournament. Your opponent has "the nuts"—the best hand possible. He covers you in chips and can knock

---

[66] Matthew 5:14-6;7:1-5;9:16-7;12:24-30;13:1-23;24-30;31-2;33-4;44;45-6;47-50;15:10-20;18:10-4;23–35;20:1-16;21:28-32;33-45;22:1-14;24:32-5;45 51,25;1-13;14-30, Mark 4:26-9, Luke 10:29-37;11:5-13;12:13-21;13:6-9;14:7-14;15:8-10;11-32;16:19-31;18:1-8;9-14, Psalms 78:2

you out. You go "all-in" thinking your strong hand is best. Your opponent's eyes widen, knowing he actually has you. Yet he just lays his hand down—folds. You eventually win, but your heart knows you didn't deserve the title. You are forever indebted. Jesus is that opponent: unselfish and competitive for us, against Himself. Loving. Amazing.

Patient & Purposeful Planner

G-d has immense and perfectly loving **patience**. His "anger lasts only a moment"; His favor, a lifetime. Jesus patiently waits, wanting all to repent before judgment day, and will keep believers from the "hour of trial." Worth the wait! Don't fret or give up on doing good. Joyfully, patiently endure evil and suffering with G-d's power and hope. Patience brings peace and is a fruit of the Spirit, so bear with and lovingly forgive one another. "Be quick to hear 👂, slow to speak 👄, slow to anger 😤." But don't be sluggish. Work heartily for G-d's kingdom, relaying His word.

G-d's perfect, faithful **purpose** prevails over our **plans**. Hearts plan courses, but G-d establishes steps. G-d formed His firm plans before existence: "plans for welfare and not for evil, to give a future and hope." G-d's plans are patient so we can completely trust and acknowledge Him. Jesus was "delivered up according to the definite plan and foreknowledge of G-d." Each human's true purpose is predestined adoption through Jesus. All creation is for G-d's purpose, including the wicked for the "day of trouble." Jesus is our plans' foundation, on which we build our lives to avert being swept away. Our plans may need "brotherly" counsel as well to succeed.[67]

---

[67] Acts 2:23, Proverbs 3:6;15:18;22;16:4;19;19:21, 1 Corinthians 13:4, James 1:19;5:8, Romans 12:12, Galatians 2:22;6:9, Ephesians 1:5;4:2, 2 Peter 3:9, Psalms 30:5;33:11, Jeremiah 29:11, Hebrews 6:12, 2 Timothy 1:9;2:4, Revelation 3:10, Colossians 3:13, Matthew 7:24-5

Pentecost's Promise of Possibility

Pentecost—Hebrew Shavuot or Feast of Harvest/Weeks—is Greek for the fiftieth day after Passover, commemorating Israel's receiving the Torah at Mt. Sinai. On the first Pentecost after Jesus ascended, the Holy Spirit, Abraham's **promised** gift to bless all nations, was sent by G-d and Jesus to all believers. We now know Abraham's "descendants," "Israel," and the "heirs of promise" are those in Jesus. The Holy Spirit of Truth came with a sound of violent wind ♠ as cloven tongues of fire rested on the apostles, filling them as they spoke in tongues. The NC of **possibility** replaced the ill-fated OC. The Holy Spirit testifies on the former. The OT: "Is anything too hard for [Yahweh]?" No. The NT: "All things are possible for one who believes." We are now empowered in the Holy Spirit.[68]

Perfect & Powerful Potter

G-d—His word, way, will, works, law, and plans—is **perfect**. Jesus, "pioneer and perfecter of faith," who by one sacrifice perfected forever those being made holy, bridged ⥉ our imperfection to G-d's perfection. In suffering, G-d perfects, confirms, strengthens, and establishes in holiness, removing body and soul contaminants until one has whole body control.

"Absolute **power** corrupts absolutely" refers to humans. G-d is infinitely perfect and powerful. G-d's power created the heavens and earth. Jesus and His gospel—the cross' † message—are the power of G-d, where faith rests, not our own wisdom. His kingdom is a matter of power, not talk. "The power of the Most High" came upon Mary as the Holy Spirit conceived Jesus. G-d's power resurrected Jesus, is in us believers, and will later resurrect us. Jesus upholds the universe by His powerful word and will take His power and

---

[68] John 16:13, Acts 2:1-4, Genesis 22:18, Jeremiah 32:27, Mark 9:23

reign soon. Boast gladly: our power is perfected in weakness and faintness, so Jesus' glorious might can rest on us. The Holy Spirit's powerful energy strengthens believers' inner beings, abounding in hope and directing what to say. The prayer of the righteous has great power as it is working. The devil has temporary, limited power: over this "dark world," with evil spiritual forces in the heavenly realms, and before Jesus, over death. Satan teaches to deny G-d's power. But Jesus gave us "authority to tread on serpents and scorpions, and over all the power of the enemy." Nothing can hurt us. We are "clothed with the power from on high," empowered beyond imagination.

G-d, our Father **Potter**, made us perfectly. His power should not be questioned. "Shall the potter be equated with the clay? That what is made would say to its maker, 'He did not make me'? Or what is formed say to him who formed it, 'He has no understanding'?"[69]

Prayer, Portion & Praise

Prayer makes requests known to G-d. Humble, thankful pleas are His incense. Entreat secretly with concise, simple words in a closed room, not boastfully. Ask the Holy Spirit what to pray for. Be watchful, ceaselessly praying full of faith and reverence, even in suffering. Pray for the big things such as leaders, wisdom, and healing, and pray for the small. Pray for yourself, the saints, and even persecutors. Jesus modeled the Lord's Prayer: "Our Father in heaven, hallowed is your name. Your kingdom come, your will be done, on earth, as it is in heaven. Give us this day our daily bread, and forgive us our debts, as we also have forgiven our debtors. And lead us not into temptation, but deliver

---

[69] Acts 1:8, James 3:2;5:16, Hebrews 1:3;2:10;14;10:14;12:2, Romans 1:16;12:2;15:13, 2 Corinthians 7:1;12:9, Psalms 18:30;19:7, Deuteronomy 32:4, Matthew 5:48, 1 Peter 5:10, Colossians 1:11;29, Ephesians 1:19;3:16;20, 1 Corinthians 1:18;24;2:4-5;4:20;6:14, Revelation 11:17, Luke 1:35;10:19;24:49, Jeremiah 32:17, 2 Timothy 3:5, Isaiah 29:16

us from evil." Never lose heart. G-d always listens! It will be yours!

Our double **portion** is G-d and Jesus. "Yahweh will inherit Judah as His portion in the holy land, and will again choose Jerusalem." Please, be our destiny, cup, and inheritance—our portion in the land of the living. Infinite **praise** for the Father and enthroned Lamb: Let all breath extol your holy names, word, glory, faithfulness, hope, goodness, steadfast love, marvels, comforts, justice, and mercies! Shout, sing, clap, and dance as a sacrifice of praise! Our hearts leap for joy and percuss from our inmost beings![70]

Peaceful Propitiator

The G-d of **peace** ♠, Prince of Peace ♦, and gospel of peace ♥ have an otherworldly completeness, shalom, which surpasses all understanding. G-d made peace with all through Jesus' blood on the cross. Jesus had to regain G-d's favor as **propitiator**, averting the Father's wrath by offering Himself to atone for all sins across all time and the whole world. Now all we need is justifying faith. G-d's peace guards hearts and minds in Jesus. Peace is the Spirit's fruit. Unity in the Spirit bonds us in peace. Children of G-d make peace.[71]

Prophet & Priest

Prophets spoke G-d's words through the Holy Spirit. Moses said, "Yahweh, your G-d, will raise for you a prophet like me from among you, from your brothers—it is to Him you shall listen": Jesus. In the OT, G-d tested with false

---

[70] Psalms 16:5;28:7;47:1;56:4;73:26;95:1-2;100:1;5;101:1;103:1;141:2;145:3;150:1-6, Ephesians 1:14;6:8;18, Matthew 5:44;6:5-13;21:22, 1 Thessalonians 5:16-7, Philippians 4:6-7, James 1:5;5:16, Romans 8:26, 1 Timothy 2:1, Revelation 5:13, Isaiah 25:1;61:7, 2 Corinthians 1:3, 1 Peter 1:3, Hebrews 13:15, Numbers 18:20, Zechariah 2:12

[71] Romans 5:1;16:20, Ephesians 3:17-9;4:3;6:15, 1 Peter 3:11, Philippians 4:7;9, Galatians 5:22, Romans 5:1, Matthew 5:9, Isaiah 9:6, Colossians 1:20.1 John 2:2

prophets who filled with vain hopes, instructed following previously unknown gods, and prophesied untrue visions in G-d's name. The NT warns of Satan's disguised servants: false prophets, teachers, apostles, christs. And a man of lawlessness will call himself G-d and reside in G-d's temple. There are also people of the "synagogue of Satan" who pretend to be Jews. They all have the appearance of godliness and will perform great signs and wonders to lead many astray, including believers. But they will deny G-d's power and bring destructive heresies onto their swift destruction. Hold firm. Be careful! Remember, Jesus was sent by G-d, and good trees bear only good fruit; diseased ones, only bad. Prophecy is a superior spiritual gift which is for both un/believers and builds up the Church.

Priests guarded knowledge, instructing others as messengers from Yahweh of Hosts. High priests were appointed to "act on behalf of men in relation to G-d, to offer gifts and sacrifices for sins," and to teach between holy/common, and un/clean. The priest's blessing places Yahweh's name on the receiver: "May Yahweh bless you and keep you; May Yahweh's face shine on you and be gracious to you; May Yahweh lift up His face toward you and give you peace."

Mysterious Melchizedek, "king of righteousness" and "peace," was G-d's first priest. He blessed Abraham and gave him bread and wine. Abraham initiated tithing by giving him a tenth of his spoils. Melchizedek's eternal order predated Levi's temporary order of Aaron. The Levites ministered the OC; it and the Law which established it were unattainable perfection. Melchizedek has no parents or genealogy: "Without beginning of days or end of life, resembling the Son of G-d, he remains a priest forever." Jesus is the last High Priest, ordained by G-d's oath, in Melchizedek's superior order, and is the NC's guarantor. Jesus, too, was not a Levite, and gave "bread" and "wine." Jesus didn't need to sacrifice for His own sins before doing it for ours; He even purified and refined the Levites. Because Jesus is eternal, His is the last blood sacrifice needed in the heavenly tabernacle sanctuary, which He built and ministers in. Upon Jesus' death, the veil partition to the holiest of holies tore, and He became our anchored forerunner to G-d's presence. Believers are "living stones ... being built up as a spiritual house for a holy priesthood to offer up spiritual sacrifices acceptable to G-d through Jesus Christ."[72]

Provider & Preserver

Abraham called G-d "Yahweh Jireh," "Yahweh will **provide**," for giving an alternative sacrifice to his son. G-d provides escapes from all temptation, for self-sufficiency, and for every bodily need. He is the Father to the fatherless and protector of widows. G-d sustained our souls by sacrificing His Son Jesus exactly where Isaac was bound. We lack nothing! Our cups overflow! G-d and His precepts **preserve** us in lovingkindness and truth. He used Noah to preserve all of humanity. He used Joseph to preserve Jacob's family—Jesus' line—among many nations. He preserved Israel through exile until Jesus came. He preserves believers' lives and souls forever.[73]

Purity

Pure hearts are unblemished, unmixed, and undefiled by the world and Satan. They have refined, controlled, and holy spirits, and are innocent, blameless, clean, and shining . Jesus said, "Blessed are the pure in heart, for they will see G-d" in His kingdom. Souls are purified in obedience to

---

[72] 1 John 4:1-3, 2 Peter 2:1, Matthew 7:17;24:24, Deuteronomy 13:3;18:15-22, Jeremiah 23:16, 2 Thessalonians 2:3-4, Revelation 3:9, Hebrews 7-9, Malachi 2:7, Ezekiel 44:23 , 1 Corinthians 12:10;14:4

[73] Philippians 4:19, Psalms 23:1;40:11;68:5;107:9;119:93, Genesis 22:13-4;50:20, 1 Corinthians 10:13, 2 Timothy 3:17, Isaiah 25:4, 2 Peter 2:5, Hebrews 10:39, Isaiah 49:6

the truth and hope in Jesus. They display sincere brotherly love. Baptism's pure water cleanses bodies. Hearts are sprinkled clean of evil consciences by Jesus' blood. G-d's word, wisdom, and commands are pure. The church must present itself to Jesus as a pure virgin. Pure religion is visiting orphans and widows in their affliction and staying unstained from the world. Gracious words are pure, but impure hearts are deceitful, disingenuous, and double-minded.[74]

---

[74] James 1:27;4:8, Matthew 5:8, 1 John 3:3, 1 Peter 1:22, 2 Corinthians 7:1;11:2, Hebrews 9:14;10:22, Psalms 12:6;19:8, Proverbs 15:26

Quickener

Quicken means to make alive, revive from death, resurrect, or restore to a former flourishing condition. All living things have been quickened by G-d. G-d the quickener can also bring humans back from troubles, sickness, and even death ☠. G-d's Holy Spirit quickened Jesus. If His Spirit is in us, He will also quicken our mortal bodies. While the first man Adam was made a living soul, the Last Adam was made a "quickening Spirit."

Quicken yourselves towards the quickener. Don't wait. Make haste! Finish your race to get your prize. "I run in the path of Your commandments, for you have set my heart free!"[75]

---

[75] Romans 8:11, 1 Corinthians 15:45, Psalms 119:32

R  r

Rabboni, Rabbi & Ruler

Mary Magdalene and a blind man called Jesus "**Rabboni**," a **Rabbi** or masterful teacher 😊🔔 held in highest esteem and honor. Jesus is, in fact, the only Rabbi. A Jewish Pharisee **ruler**, Nicodemus, called Jesus Rabbi because he realized that Jesus is the "ruler of kings on earth," fulfilling the prophecy of a ruler of ancient times from Bethlehem who would shepherd Israel.[76]

Rain-giver of Righteousness

In proper seasons and amounts, *rain* is a kind blessing, a sustenance requirement—food itself when manna rained—and a testament to G-d's unparalleled power of creation. While withheld rain, accompanied by hail, fire, and sulfur, or flood-inducing is devastating, good rain returns along with its aftermath: G-d's bow of promise and faithfulness. G-d sends rain on the just and on the unjust. So, too, we must love and pray for our persecuting enemies. The OT's clouds showering down the word and **righteousness** sowed the NT's fruits of the Spirit and crops of G-d's kingdom. The Holy Spirit "poured out" from heaven for our vindication and salvation.

---

[76] John 3:1-2;4:31;20:16, Mark 10:51, Revelation 1:5, Micah 5:2-4

"The Righteous One" is the path to life and not death. Without Jesus "none is righteous, no, not one." In the OT, righteous people were blameless and upright under the law and faithfully obedient to G-d, "Yahweh, our **Righteousness**." In the NT, Jesus is "the righteousness from G-d that depends on faith." G-d gifted us with blessed justification by making Jesus "to be sin, who knew no sin." We can't have our own righteousness, but hunger and thirst for G-d's to be worthy of His kingdom. Righteousness carries godliness, love, purity, truth, honor, integrity, justice, and equity. A righteous harvest 🌾 sows peace and reaps love. The unrighteous are arrogant evildoers who conceal the truth and promote lawlessness and sin.[77]

Recompense of Ransomed Reward

Jesus' blood made amends, compensating for all humanity's harm, loss, and suffering. Don't worry about being repaid in this life, and don't repay evil with evil. On the last day, Jesus will bring His **recompense** from His judgment seat "to repay each one for what he has done," blessing the just and punishing the unjust. So be blessed and free. Faithfully seek and work hard for G-d and Jesus in love. Persevere and rejoice confidently through trials and persecution. "Love your enemies, do good, and lend expecting nothing in return."

Jesus released from prison in the depths or belly of Sheol/Hades all souls doomed under the law. This prison is the realm of the dead 💀 with its Abyss, a bottomless pit run by angel Abaddon or Apollyon, whose name means "destruction." Jesus paid the demanded **ransom**:

---

[77] Jeremiah 23:6, Romans 1:18;3:10;10:4, Philippians 3:9;4:8, 2 Corinthians 5:21;6:14, Matthew 5:6;45;6:33, 2 Thessalonians 1:5, Proverbs 2:7-9;8:7, Psalms 94:4, James, 3:8, Hosea 10:12, John 5:17, Revelation 9:11, Acts 14:17, Exodus 9:23;16:4, Joel 2:28; Deuteronomy 11:17, Genesis 7:4;9:13, Isaiah 44:3;45:8;53:11;55:10

His precious blood. Our bodies were bought; they are no longer our own. Now our life's work, built on the prophets, apostles, and Jesus' foundation, will be fire-tested. What survives is our **reward**; what doesn't, our loss. G-d's inheritance, kingdom, and heavenly treasure are the ultimate reward. We will receive imperishable wreaths, crowns ♛ of life, righteousness, and unfading glory. On earth, children are the reward. Pray, fast, and give to the needy secretly to avoid seeking human reward.[78]

Reconciler, Restorer & Redeemer

Jesus **reconciled** us to G-d, **restored** believers to our rightful place, and **redeemed** G-d's kingdom. While still enemies of G-d, Jesus' death reconciled us and the world to Himself. He entrusted us with the message of reconciliation—the gospel—for His ministry of reconciliation. Jesus restored mankind to its rightful, pre-disobedience connection with G-d in Eden. Jesus reconnected our image-bearing ability, which we short-circuited: the irreparable 💔 repaired ♥. Believers will suffer physically, emotionally, or spiritually, but Jesus restores, and is coming back to restore everything. Believers are also called to gently restore each other if caught in a sin. In the OT, redemption meant that if a Jew was unable to pay for his land, a close relative could step in and redeem it for him. Jesus, our brother, redeemed our souls back to the land of the living and G-d's kingdom, back as G-d our Father's own possession. The sinful debt we owed was death; the price was Jesus' blood. Jesus redeemed us from the law, our adversary Satan, and the pit of hell.[79]

---

[78] Revelation 22:12, Psalms 5:12;86:13, Colossians 3:23-4, James 1:2-4, Matthew 5:12;6:1-6;6:33, Luke 6:27-28, 1 Corinthians 3:14-15;9:24-25, 2 Timothy 4:8, James 1:12, 1 Peter 1:18-19;5:4, Galatians 2:20, 1 Timothy 2:6, Hebrews 2:9, John 8:44

[79] Romans 5:10, 2 Corinthians 5:18-21, Acts 3:21, Galatians 6:1, Ephesians 1:7, Psalms 107:2, Job 33:28, Ephesians 1:14

Remembrance & Repentance

G-d's memory 🧠 is razor sharp. He makes good on His promises—to Noah, Abraham, Rachel, Joseph, Hannah, and His covenant. G-d commands **remembrance** of Sabbath and Passover. Jesus commands that bread reminds us of His giving His body for us. To that G-d said, "I will remember their sins and their lawless deeds no more." The Holy Spirit is a remembrance of Jesus' teachings. "The memory of the righteous is a blessing" forever, but the names of evildoers, such as Amalekites, will rot, blotted from the Book of Life [Remembrance].[80]

We must always remember all G-d does, and actively turn to Him to live. **Repentance** is the direction you face, what your heart follows: G-d or anything else. If everyone repented, the second coming would already be; but, these days are like Noah and the flood. G-d is patiently waiting for as many people as possible to come to faith and be saved so that He might blot out sins and gift the Holy Spirit. Believe in the gospel and be baptized! Repentance is godly grief to confess and forsake transgressions to obtain mercy. To keep in repentance, we must bear fruit to truly be Abraham's blessed descendants. We must forgive each time a believer repents. Jesus' return will wage war against the unrepentant with the sword of His mouth, "removing [their] lampstand from its place" and trampling them underfoot.[81]

Revealer & Resurrector

G-d self-**revealed** through His Spirit deep things about His Kingdom and His mystery in Jesus and the gospel: that Gentiles can be fellow heirs by faith. Be humble and

---

[80] Genesis 8:1;19:29;30:22;41:9, 1 Samuel 1:19, Exodus 2:24;20:8;12:14, Psalms 105:8, Luke 22:19-20, Jeremiah 31:34, John 14:26, Proverbs 10:7, Malachi 3:16
[81] Ezekiel 18:32, 2 Peter 3:9, Acts 3:19;2:38, Isaiah 44:22, 2 Corinthians 7:9-10, Proverbs 28:13, Luke 3:8;17:3-4, Revelation 2:16;3:19, Matthew 24:37

resilient—G-d reveals more to "little children" than the "wise and learned." And "our present sufferings are not worth comparing with the glory that will be revealed in us. For the creation waits in eager expectation for the children of G-d to be revealed." Jesus' Revelation foretells the Apocalypse, when G-d will disclose all His plan's secrets and shed His light 💡 on the hidden or darkened, including the purposes of the heart and the relationship between Jesus and His Church.

"I am the **resurrection** and the life. Whoever believes in me, though he die, yet he will live, and everyone who lives and believes in me will never die." Jesus tasted death so we don't have to forever gorge. He lords over the dead and living through this age and the next. Our baptism shares in Jesus' experience: dying to sin underwater and emerging alive again in G-d. We will be like Jesus when He returns, and we will see Him as He is if we share in His suffering. The same Spirit which resurrected Jesus can dwell in our mortal bodies so we only "fall asleep." Jesus will resurrect everyone in G-d's power and glory on the last day—the just to everlasting life; the unjust to judgment, shame, and everlasting contempt. Jesus will descend, and those dead in Jesus will rise first. "Awake and sing for joy!"[82]

Rock & Refuge

"G-d is my **Rock** 🪨, in whom I take **refuge**," our salvation and shelter. Reliable, everlasting, and mighty. The most intimate human encounter with G-d was Moses hiding in the cleft of a rock while Yahweh's goodness passed by. Moses saw Yahweh's back. Anyone, save Jesus, who saw G-d's face would die. The Israelites ate spiritual food—manna— and drank spiritual water. The water-providing rock was

---

[82] John 5:29;11:25-26, Hebrews 2:9, Romans 1:17;6:4;10-11;8:18-9;14:9, Titus 3:5, Colossians 2:12, 1 John 3:2, 1 Thessalonians 4:13-18, Isaiah 26:19, 1 Corinthians 2:2;10;4:5, Ephesians 3:3-6;5:32, Luke 12:2, Matthew 11:25

actually Jesus. Jesus is the "tested, precious cornerstone" on which we should build our lives to weather all storms. On His Rock, we are above our troubles. He was also the living stone rejected by men, but in the sight of G-d chosen and precious. Contrarily, the law was a "stumbling stone" and "rock of offense" because it couldn't be kept.[83]

Root

Jesus is the **root** of Jesse and David. "If the root is holy, the branches are too." Those who trust, meditate, delight, and are rooted in the love of G-d and Jesus are blessed like an evergreen, fruit-producing tree by a stream. No need for fear or anxiety. But "roots of bitterness" stir trouble and defile, and love of money is the "root of all kinds of evil." These roots will be pulled out and burnt.[84]

---

[83] Psalms 18:2;89:26, Deuteronomy 32:15, Isaiah 26:4;28:16, 1 Corinthians 10:4, Matthew 7:24-25, 1 Peter 2:4

[84] Isaiah 11:10, Romans 11:16, Psalms 1:1-3, Jeremiah 17:7-8, Ephesians 3:16-19, Revelation 5:5, Hebrews 12:15, 1 Timothy 6:10

Sabbath, Stillness & Shiloh

Jesus is Lord of **Sabbath**—Hebrew for "cease" or "rest." He rested when "it was very good" after creation. Yet Jesus Incarnate never rested from good works: He healed a cripple, an invalid, a shriveled hand, and allowed His apostles to "work" for food. "My Father is always at His work, to this very day, and I too am working." Sabbath is an everlasting covenant, but "was made for man," not vice versa. So enter G-d's solemn rest. Be refreshed. *Sleep zzz*. Honor and delight in the holy day. "Yahweh will fight for you, you need only" "be **still**, and know that [He is] G-d." Cease from going your way, seeking your pleasures, and talking idly. Profaning Sabbath in bad works or doing worldly work both bring punishments of death and cutting a soul off from the "holy nation." Jesus is "**Shiloh**," the "Peaceful One," from Jacob's blessing of Judah: "My peace I give you. I do not give you as the world gives." "I will give you rest."[85] Hold your peace!

Sanctifying Source of Sainthood

Sanctification makes **saints**, who have been returned to their **source**. Sanctification is G-d's sharing His holiness

---

[85] Luke 6:15 10,13:16, Mark 2:27, John 5:8, Matthew 11:28-30, Isaiah 58:13, Ezekiel 20:14, Exodus 14:14;31:14, Psalms 46:10, Hebrews 4:9-11

to make us clean and unblemished. In the OT, keeping G-d's statutes like Sabbath was the sign of G-d's sanctifying Israel, separating them for His special purposes of being His holy nation and proclaiming His excellence. Now faith in Jesus and the word leads to sanctification and its end, eternal life, by the Holy Spirit's fruits. Believers perform their proper human function and G-d's will, becoming useful to our Master as His own possession, pre-chosen elect, royal priesthood, holy nation Israel, and Jesus' saints—"most holy things" in Greek. Jesus' perfect blood sacrifice sanctifies His church for all time, is what saves, and is how we can see Jesus. Remaining holy is to be G-d-fearing and in control of our bodies, avoiding sexual immorality. When G-d's sanctuary, Holy Place, is among us forever, the nations will know that G-d has sanctified Israel. Those sanctified and the Sanctifier come from the same source. We really are Jesus' brothers and sisters, with no human divisions of religion, race, gender, or nationality. We are one in G-d, in one Spirit, baptized into one body.

Blood ⟨⟩—and the heart—is the source of life, which is why we don't eat it of animals. Jesus is the source of eternal life because of His blood. G-d is the source of everything, but specifically light, glory, well-being, strength, encouragement, endurance, joy, hope, lovingkindness, sustenance, living water, stability, security, honor, pride, confidence, and wealth—all attained permanently in Jesus.[86]

Satan-Smiter

Our enemies are not flesh and blood. The real fight is an epic invisible battle of good vs. evil, light vs. dark, G-d vs.

---

[86] Leviticus 20:8;21:8, Acts 3:15;26:18, 2 Thessalonians 2:13, 2 Timothy 2:21, John 17:17, 1 Thessalonians 4:3-4, Hebrews 2:11;5:9;10:4;12:2,14, 1 Peter 2:9, 2 Corinthians 7:1;13:11, Ezekiel 37:28, 1 Corinthians 12:23, Deuteronomy 12:23, 1 Chronicles 16:27;29:12, Psalms 16:2;47:4;71:5;119:57. Proverbs 4:23, Isaiah 20:6;33:6;60:15;60:19; Jeremiah 2:13, Zechariah 2:5, Romans 6:22;15:13

Satan 😼, two fathers grappling for all children. G-d will soon win. Satan tempted G-d's Son Jesus, who emerged victorious by debunking Satan with Scripture. Jesus' incarnation destroyed Satan's work, sin. Jesus' return will save believers, destroy death, and imprison Satan in permanent torment.

Know thy enemy. Satan—the devil, evil one, ancient serpent, day star, son of dawn—is our crafty and cunning "adversary," tempting with incremental sinful practice. He accuses and shames us repeatedly as we try to cover up mistakes. Give him no opportunity. Satan tries to hinder good works and godly gathering. He instigates impulsivity and greed, dealing in flesh alone. "The Father of Lies" fills hearts to lie to G-d and the Holy Spirit; lying is his native language. His children practice lawlessness and unrighteousness, not loving others, and hating the light. Satan instills murderous desires since he "was a murderer [and sinner] from the beginning." Satan and his spiritual army of bad angels steal people to a burning destruction, robbing of salvation. Scheming Satan tricks and deceives the whole world, which he controls. He constantly prowls to devour. He wants to trap and sift us so we fall to his level to do his will. Every bad human action is Satan's doing. He attacks, oppresses, weakens, and binds through suffering with his fiery arrows, causing crippling or illness. Satan opposes peace with conflict, disharmony, and disruption. He is "the author of confusion." "The G-d of Peace" will crush him underfoot. Satan pretends to be god, father, powerful ruler, prince, lion, star, and angel of light with his angel legion, yet he is nothing like G-d the Father, the Powerful Ruler and Prince, the Lion, the Morning Star, and G-d's angels. Put on G-d's armor and be a warrior to withstand him (see "W"). Submit to G-d; resist Satan, and he will flee you. Satan, get behind us; we rebuke you! Even demons believe there is one G-d and shudder! The Spirit and angels will attend to us as they did after Jesus was tempted. Jesus granted power over the enemy, and G-d has given endurance and an escape from every temptation.[87]

Shepherd & Savior

"Yahweh is my **shepherd**—I lack nothing." In the OT, G-d foreshadowed Jesus' parable of seeking the one lost sheep: Lot in Sodom, Joseph in Egypt, and Rahab in Jericho. In incredibly sinful cities facing annihilation, G-d spared the faithful loner along with his or her families. Then G-d sent Jesus, the Chief and Good Shepherd, for the shepherdless and straying sheep—Jew, then Gentile. He was "struck" and laid "down His life for the sheep." About His "little flock" of believers, Jesus said, "I know them [by name], and they know me." Jesus' "good pasture" is beyond physical: He is the shepherd and "overseer of our souls." "He will gather the lambs in His arms; He will carry them in His bosom, and gently lead those that are young" to the "springs of living water." Jesus leads but also comes alongside as the Lamb of G-d. We must also "feed" and "tend" fellow sheep. But beware of wolves, including false prophets in sheep's clothing.

The gospel of salvation begins, "Today in the town of David ✡, a **Savior** has been born to you; He is the Messiah, the Lord." G-d fulfilled raising a Savior from David for Israel by incarnating His Son to wholly save each human and the world from sinful evil. Jesus' very name means "salvation," "saving people from their sins."[88]

---

[87] Ephesians 6:11-16, Romans 16:20, Revelation 12:9-10;20:2, James 2:19;4:7, 1 John 3:8,10, Acts 5:3;10:38, John 8:44;10:10;12:31, 2 Timothy 2:26, Matthew 4:1-11, 1 Peter 5:8, 2 Corinthians 11:3,14, Luke 10:19;11:18;13:16;22:31, Hebrews 2:14, Isaiah 14:12, Zechariah 3:2, 1 Corinthians 10:13

[88] Psalms 23:1, John 10:1-42;21:17, 1 Peter 2:25;5:4, Isaiah 40:11, Revelation 7:17, Zechariah 13:7, Luke 2:11;12:32;15:4-7, Matthew 1:21;7:17;10:16, Hebrews 7:25, 1 John 4:14, Acts 13:23, Titus 2:13

Shutter & Sealer

Staying with G-d in Jesus encloses us in love and protection. "If [G-d] **shuts** a man in, none can open." Jesus "shuts and no one opens." Circumcision was G-d's **seal**. Then G-d set His seal on Jesus. G-d establishes in Jesus, anoints, seals like a signet ring His and Jesus' names on foreheads, and pledges the Holy Spirit to hearts. The Holy Spirit seals for the day of redemption. "But G-d's firm foundation stands, bearing this seal: 'The Lord knows those who are His' and 'Let everyone who names the name of the Lord depart from iniquity.'" But if we the Church bride aren't ready for Jesus the bridegroom's marriage return, the door will shut, as will the pit. Judgment and harm will befall those without G-d's seal.[89]

Son, Servant & Sacrifice

Jesus is the one and only **Son** of the living G-d, the Father Most High. He is the radiance of G-d's glory, heir of all things, the exact imprint of G-d "who is Himself G-d," and in the closest relationship with the Father. G-d loves Jesus with whom His soul is well pleased, and He has given all things into His hand. Jesus is the Son of Man, fulfilling the prophecy of a child born, a son given. He is the son of Mary and Joseph, from David's line. Jesus felt the full human experience—despised, rejected, a "man of sorrows and acquainted with grief" who "has borne our griefs and carried our sorrows," and allowed Himself to be wounded to heal us.

Believers were predestined by G-d to be adopted, in love, into the Sonship alongside Jesus and led by the Spirit. No longer slaves, but heirs, we are children of light and

---

[89] Job 12:14, 2 Corinthians 1:21-2, 1 Timothy 2:19, Revelation 3:7,9:4;14:1, Ezekiel 9:1-11, Matthew 25:10, Luke 1:32|13:25;19:10, Psalms 69:15, John 6:27, Ephesians 1:13; 4:30, Romans 4:11

day. The Spirit bears witness with our spirits that we are children of G-d. The Father disciplined His perfect Son instead of us. He disciplines us children to better us.

Moses had the highest human title, "**servant** of G-d." David was also a "servant." "For even the Son of Man did not come to be served, but to serve." G-d raised His chosen servant: Jesus could have put Himself on equal footing with G-d—"in Him the whole fullness of deity dwells bodily"— but He didn't. Jesus said, "The Father is greater than I." Jesus humbly emptied Himself to human likeness, taking the nature of servant of G-d, but then became a servant of us too. He said that His food was G-d's will. To be a "servant of Christ," one dutifully follows Him, works heartily, takes up the cross daily, and is not people-pleasing. Yet Jesus calls us friends, not servants, because He has shared the Master's plans. Jesus' servants were given His revelation to know what is to come. Be a "servant of G-d" by being equipped with Scripture. Work to hear "well done, good and faithful servant" by lovingly serving fellow believers and others, sharing as "good stewards" G-d's various gifts. "Wash each other's feet" 📖. Last will be first: humbled, exalted; "bondservants" freed. Authorities, including taxing, should be obeyed as "G-d's servants."

Jesus humbled Himself twice: first as a human-like servant, then to death on the cross—our atoning, fragrant **sacrifice**. In Jesus, praising G-d, "the fruit of lips that openly profess His name," is a sacrifice. Spiritual worship, good deeds, self-sacrificial love, and sharing with others are "living" sacrifices holy, acceptable, and pleasing to G-d. G-d desired Jesus' body, not animal sacrifices. From us, G-d desires "righteousness and justice"; a broken spirit; and a "broken, contrite heart." The two greatest commandments encompass love, knowledge of G-d, and obedience. But, deliberately sinning undoes Jesus' sacrifice, and pagans sacrifice to demons.⁹⁰

Sovereign Shade, Shelter & Shield

G-d alone **sovereignly** does as He pleases. When lots are cast 🎲, G-d still decides. He declared the "end from the beginning": "He will swallow up death forever. The sovereign Yahweh will wipe away the tears from all faces. He will remove His people's disgrace from all the earth." Jesus holds all things together: "The Spirit of sovereign Yahweh is on [Jesus] because Yahweh has anointed [Him] to proclaim good news to the poor. He has sent [Jesus] to bind up the brokenhearted, to proclaim freedom for the captives and release from darkness for the prisoners." Humans humbly exist for G-d's purpose. But G-d is pleased to love and protect those who proclaim His glory. G-d provides merciful **shade** from the heat, **shelter** under His wings from trouble-storms and strife of tongues, and **shields** from enemy attacks. "Whoever dwells in the shelter of the Most High will rest in the shadow of the Almighty." We excitedly await to take shade under the Tree of Life. G-d's favor covers the righteous with a shield. The shield of faith extinguishes the fiery arrows Satan shoots at us—who casts a deep, dark "shadow of death."⁹¹

Spirit

G-d's **Spirit** permeates the OT. At creation the Spirit hovered over the expanse of water before the world took

---

⁹⁰ John 1:18;3:35;4:34;12:16;13:1-17;14:28;15:15, Romans 3:25;8:14;16;12:1, Hebrews 1:2-3;10:5;12:7, Ephesians 1:5;5:1-2, Galatians 1:10;4:7;5:13, Mark 10:45;12:13, Matthew 16:16, Luke 3:22;9:23;17:10, 1 Thessalonians 5:5, 2 Timothy 3:16-7, Philippians 2:6-8, Colossians 3:23-4, 1 Peter 4:10, Isaiah 53:1-12;42:1, Acts 3:26, 1 Corinthians 7:22;10:20, Proverbs 21:3, Hosea 6:6, Psalms 51:17, 1 Samuel 15:22, Revelation 1:1
⁹¹ Psalms 5:12;27:5;31:20;115:5;36:7;61:4;91:1;121:5, Isaiah 4:6;24:4-5;25:8;46:10;61:1, Daniel 4:2, Ezekiel 17:23; Ephesians 1:11;6:16, 1 Timothy 6:15, Deuteronomy 4:39, Romans 8:28, Colossians 1:17, Proverbs 16:33

form. Before the flood Yahweh said His Spirit would "not contend with humans forever, for they are mortal; their days will be a hundred and twenty years." Joseph 🐃 had the "Spirit of G-d." Moses shared the Spirit within him with seventy elders to lessen his leadership burden. The Spirit of God fell upon Bezalel and his fellow tabernacle architects and filled them with wisdom and workmanship. Because Caleb had a different spirit, he alone from his generation entered Israel. Joshua was "a man whom the Spirit is in," and Moses gave him the Spirit of wisdom. All prophets spoke from G-d through His "generous" Spirit.

"And the Spirit of Yahweh will rest upon Him, the Spirit of wisdom and understanding, the Spirit of counsel and might, the Spirit of knowledge, and the fear of the Lord." When Jesus was baptized, heaven opened, and G-d's dove-like 🕊 Spirit rested on Him. Jesus sacrificed Himself through the eternal Spirit. "Father, into your hands, I commit My Spirit." After Jesus was raised by G-d's Spirit, He breathed on people and said, "Receive the Holy Spirit." Jesus is now the "Spirit of Christ," and believers are transforming into that glorious image. After Jesus ascended to heaven, the Father sent the Holy Spirit—Ru'ach HaKodesh or Agio Pnevma—in Jesus' name at the Pentecost. The Holy Spirit is the promise of Abraham's seed, Jesus, through which all nations are blessed, "whether Jews or Gentiles, slave or free." We are all given the "one Spirit to drink" for a guaranteed inheritance. The Holy Spirit poured out G-d's love into believers' hearts, giving full meaning to "not by might, not by power, but by my Spirit." The Spirit of holiness gives power to inner beings so Jesus can live in faithful hearts. The Spirit transforms fearful slaves into adopted children, fulfilling us in G-d's will by renewing and regenerating hearts and spirits. G-d's Spirit—Our Teacher, Advocate, Helper, and Interceder in weakness—will even tell us what to speak or pray when we don't know. As such, our bodies have been bought, no longer our own, but have become temples for the Holy Spirit. Live for the Spirit who gives eternal life and peace, not the flesh which brings death and destruction. "For G-d gave us a Spirit not of fear [or timidity], but of power and love and self-control" and hope. Speak the word of G-d boldly. Only G-d's Spirit knows His thoughts; we pray for the "Spirit of wisdom and revelation" and "grace" to know G-d better. But to resist the Holy Spirit is to be "stiff-necked" and "uncircumcised in heart and ears." And blaspheming the Spirit is the only unforgivable sin.

Ministers of the NC gain competency from G-d's Spirit. Our perfect Father gives the good gift of His Spirit to those who ask and are baptized with water and His Spirit. G-d's children are obediently led by G-d's Spirit, blessed to enter G-d's kingdom. The Spirit of Truth himself testifies to it. The Spirit's fruits bring personal growth: "Love, joy, peace, patience, kindness, goodness, faithfulness, gentleness, and self-control. Against such things there is no law."[92]

Strength, Song & Salvation

Moses and Miriam sang after G-d split the Red Sea: ♪ "Yahweh is my **strength** and my **song**, and He has become my **salvation**." Yahweh puts on strength as if it were His belt. He and His word renew His hopeful people's strength to not grow weary or faint. He is our heart and souls' strength and makes our feet like a deer's to tread on the heights. We can do anything! Jesus strengthens and protects from the devil if we seek His face always. We become strong in grace, trust, and quietness: "When I am weak, then I am strong." In turn, we must love G-d with whole heart, soul, mind, and strength. We can impart G-d's gift of strength with

---

[92] Exodus 28:3, Hebrews 9:14;10:29, Luke 11:13;23:46, Romans 5:5;8:6;11-16;26-7;15:13, Ephesians 1:17;3:16-7, 1 Corinthians 2:11;6:19-20;12:13, Galatians 5:17;22-3;6:8, 1 Timothy 1:7, Zechariah 4:6, Acts 2:38;4:31;5:32;7:51, 2 Corinthians 3:18, Mark 13:11, 2 Peter 1:21, Ezekiel 36.26, Matthew 12:31, John 3:5;14:26;16:13;20:22, Nehemiah 9:20, Numbers 14:24, Titus 3:5

mutual encouragement in faith. We can also strongly shout out loud when cheerful. Sing melodies old and new from the Spirit. Sing praise of G-d's might, marvel, and wonder from a thankful heart until the new song of the Lamb plays. G-d surrounds us with "songs of deliverance." "The sound of joyful shouting and salvation is in the tents of the righteous." Only with baptism in Jesus—faithfully keeping His commandments and believing the gospel that Jesus is Lord and was raised from the dead—is eternal salvation found. Call on His name. G-d's grace works within those who fearfully do His will to save all souls. We must bring "salvation to the ends of the earth" by sharing the gospel. Jesus' purpose in returning is to save those awaiting Him.[93]

Spiritual-Sufficiency & All-Seer

The Omniscient and "All-**Sufficient** One"—G-d—**sees** all, rewards good done in secrecy, and provides all we need. "And my G-d will supply every need of yours according to His riches in glory in Christ Jesus." G-d's grace makes believers "sufficient in all things at all times," "lacking in nothing." Scripture makes a "man of G-d" "complete, equipped in every good work." "His divine power has given us everything we need for a godly life through our knowledge of Him who called us by His own glory and goodness": Jesus. G-d will never allow us to be tempted beyond our ability: sufficient roots will not wither. He is always looking to provide "suitable helpers" for our benefit, be they friends, family, or a spouse. Most lovingly, G-d made us sufficient for redemption with Jesus. In turn, believers should be good stewards by serving each other with their varied gifts of G-d's grace and sharing with the poor. There is no need for anxiety. G-d will meet

---

[93] Isaiah 30:15;40:31;41:10, Psalms 32:7;69:30;71:23;73:26;95:1;98:1;118:15;119:28;138:3;150:2, Philippians 2:12;4:13, I Chronicles 16:11, 2 Thessalonians 3:3, Habakkuk 3:19, Mark 12:30, 2 Timothy 2:1, Romans 1:11-2;16;10:9;13, 2 Corinthians 12:10, Ephesians 2:8-9;5:19, Revelation 5:9, James 5:13, Titus 2:11, Acts 4:12;13:47;28:28, I Peter 1:9, Hebrews 9:28, Matthew 7:21

our needs for sustenance, protection, shelter, clothing, and energy. Don't look elsewhere, or you will try to hide it. "There is no creature hidden from His sight, all are naked and exposed." "Darkness [and secret sin] is as light" to Him. His understanding is beyond measure. He knows every plan and thought. Yahweh's eyes are everywhere "keeping watch on the evil and the good." We should pray in quiet solitude, hide fasting, and give to the needy quietly. Remember, G-d fills the heaven and earth and sees the inside of the cup ☕, "the secrets of the heart" and mind. Jesus already knows who will be believers. Their lives are hidden, tucked away in Him. Apocalypse means everything hidden will become evident, and everything secret will become known and come to light.[94]

Sun & Star

Yahweh is a **sun**—warmth, light, and very survival. The sun shines on evil and good, until after the tribulation, when the sun will become black. G-d will literally replace the sun. Jesus' face will shine like the sun. "The righteous will shine like the sun in the kingdom of their Father." All will be healed and illuminated. Jesus will return as the sun ☼ and a star ✦. "A **star** will come out of Jacob." With Jesus' birth, His star rose into the sky. When Jesus returns He will be the "bright morning star."

Sword & Staff

The **sword** of the Spirit is the word of G-d. Jesus will return a warrior, "from His mouth, a two-edged sword," will strike

---

[94] Philippians 4:19, 2 Corinthians 9:8;12:9, 2 Peter 1:3, 2 Timothy 1:7;16-17, Colossians 3:2, Genesis 2:18, Deuteronomy 15:8, Psalms 44:21;46:1;90:8;139:12;147:5, Isaiah 13:5;23:18, Matthew 6:1;13:5, 1 Peter 4:10; James, 1:4, Hebrews 4:13, Proverbs 15:3, 1 Chronicles 28:9, Jeremiah 23:24, Revelation 2:23, John 6:64, Luke 8:17

down the nations; all wrongdoing avenged; complete conquest; war no more. Jesus will beat evil into submission with Judah's scepter and an iron ruler's rod. Then a measuring rod will measure the new temple, altar, and Jerusalem. The shepherd's "rod and **staff** †, they comfort me."[95]

---

[95] Psalms 2:9;23:4;84:11, Revelation 1:16;2:1,27;11:1;16;19:15;22:5;16, Matthew 2:1-2;5:45;13:43, John 8:12, Malachi 4:2, Numbers 24:17, Ephesians 6:17, Isaiah 2:4, Genesis 49:10

Thanksgivings: Testimony & Tithe

Rejoice, pray, and **give thanks** in all circumstances. This is G-d's will. Be wholeheartedly thankful to be in G-d's presence and to receive an unshakeable kingdom. Submit requests through thankful prayers, petitions, and intercessions for all people, and receive G-d's peace, steadfast love, strength, and grace in Jesus. Give thanks to G-d through Jesus in everything you do— word, deed, or song. It is a sacrifice to magnify G-d's glory. Everything G-d created is good, to be received with thanksgiving. We will proclaim thanks when Jesus begins His reign. Praise and "thanks be to G-d." Two outward displays of thankfulness in Jesus are **testimonies** and **tithes**.

G-d and His Spirit testify to Jesus. We must sanctify Jesus as Lord in our hearts, standing ready to gently and respectfully confess our personal defense of hope, our testimony, even unto death. When the gospel of the kingdom is preached to all nations as testimony— that "G-d has given us eternal life, and this life is in His Son"— the end will come ♥. Acknowledge Jesus, and He will acknowledge you to His Father and the angels. Deny Him, and be denied.

Abraham tithed a tenth of his spoils. Jacob promised back ten percent of all G-d gave him. The Israelites tithed to the Levites. Cheerful, willing, and quiet tithing for G-d's kingdom is the law. Honor Yahweh with every tenth, which is holy. Test G-d with full-tithing; see G-d open heaven's windows to pour down overflowing blessings.[96]

Tower & Torch

G-d provides safety out of His burning love. Yahweh is "a **tower** of strength against the enemy." Physical towers, like Babel 𝄞, will all fall. Then, towering, heavenly new Jerusalem will come. "I will not keep silent because of Zion, and I will not keep still because of Jerusalem, until her righteousness shines like a light, her salvation like a flaming **torch** 🔥." G-d introduced Himself to Moses as the burning bush, and the Holy Spirit first manifested as divided fiery tongues. "The Light of Israel will become a fire; their Holy One a flame." Jesus will return, eyes aglow "like a flame of fire," on His throne with the torches of G-d's Seven Spirits. Have white-hot hearts for G-d and Jesus, not lukewarm. Fan into flame G-d's gifted salvation. And keep your lamps lit![97]

Treasured Tester of Truth

"For where your **treasure** 💰 is, there your heart will also be." Be rich in good deeds and toward G-d to enter His kingdom! Treasure G-d's words over food! Fear, wisdom, knowledge of G-d, Jesus' mystery, and the Holy Spirit are entrusted treasures: our *trophies*! G-d's treasured possession is "Israel," Jesus' believers. So tithe and stand ready to share. Fill unaging moneybags, not living for worldly, failing "riches,"

---

[96] Genesis 14:20;28:22, Leviticus 27:32, 1 Thessalonians 5:16-18, Hebrews 12:28, Psalms 3:9;9:1;28:7;69:30;95:2;107:8, Philippians 4:6, Colossians 3:17, 2 Corinthians 2:14;4:15;9:7, 1 Timothy 1:12;2:1;4:4-5;6:12, 1 Corinthians 1:4, Revelation 6:9;11:17, Daniel 2:23, 1 John 5:6-11, Matthew 23:23;24:14, 1 Peter 3:15, Luke 12:8-9, Malachi 3:10

[97] Proverbs 18:10, Genesis 11:4-5, Zechariah 14:10, Psalms 48:3, Revelation 2:18;4:5, Isaiah 10:17;33:6;62:1, Exodus 3:2, 2 Timothy 1:6, Acts 2:1-4, Daniel 7:9, Proverbs 11:4, Ezekiel 7:19, Luke 24:32

destroyed by moths and rust, stolen by thieves. They will not profit on the day of wrath. Good people bring forth good from their good treasures; same for evil. Understanding and wisdom are better than silver or gold. G-d's true treasury holds weather, rain, sleet, hail, snow, lightning, and wind, not precious metals and gems.

G-d and His Word are the **truth**—which is where love rejoices. Jesus said, "I am the way and the truth and the life." Know the truth about G-d, His Son, and His Spirit of truth, and be set free. Correctly handle the Word of Truth—the gospel of salvation. Speak from the heart, walk in, live out, worship in, and be led by the truth. Wear the "belt of truth." Don't be harsh, but don't lie.

Yahweh **tests** righteous minds and hearts to hold onto the truth. G-d tested Abraham. Israel received manna as "daily bread" ⤳ to test keeping G-d's commands: they failed, testing G-d ten times. Jesus tested the disciple Philip in procuring food for five thousand. Faith refined in the fiery furnace of affliction builds endurance, authenticity, steadfastness, and discernment of "G-d's will—what is good, acceptable, and perfect." Jesus is the smelter. Count trials a joy. Test all spirits, prophets, apostles, and dreamers to determine if from G-d or the antichrist. Self-examine to faithfully keep Jesus' word, and He will remain in you and spare you from the coming "hour of trial" on earth. "Do not put Yahweh, your G-d to the test," save whole-tithing.[98]

Trinity: Time, Teacher & Tongues

Baptism is in the names of the Father, Son, and the Holy Spirit—the Holy **Trinity**. They are all G-d and all one in

---

[98] Romans 12:2, Hebrews 11:17, 1 John 1:6;4:1-4;6:5-6, James 1:2-3;12, 1 Peter 1:7, Psalms 11:5;15:3;26:2, Zechariah 13:9, Malachi 3:3;10, Exodus 16:4, Numbers 14:22; Deuteronomy 6:16;13:3;14:2;28:12, 2 Corinthians 13:5, 1 Corinthians 3:13;16:6, Revelation 2:2;3:10, Isaiah 48:10, John 4:24;8:32;14:6;15:26, Ephesians 1:13;4:15;6:14, 2 Timothy 1:13;2:15, Matthew 6:19 21;12:35;13:44, Proverbs 2:4-5;16:16, Luke 12:21;33, 1 Timothy 6:18-9, Colossians 2:2-3, Job 23:12, Joshua 6:19

G-d's will, yet three entities. "For there are three that testify: the Spirit, and the water, and the blood; and these three agree." Biblical phrases repeated thrice, like "Holy, Holy, Holy!", are paramount. May G-d's love, Jesus' grace and the Holy Spirit's fellowship be with you!

Father **Time:** time and seasons are fixed by G-d's authority, not ours. "My times are in your hand" "as long as days are 'days.'" "The times of ignorance G-d overlooked, but now He commands all people everywhere to repent." Only G-d knows the time of the second coming.

Brother **Teacher:** Jesus is the only rabbi and rabboni because He is intimately connected to the Word and perfectly aligned to G-d's will. The Holy Spirit reminds us of Jesus' teachings. Disciples must baptize and teach others Jesus' commandments. But teachers get "greater strictness."

Helper **Tongues** 👅: the Holy Spirit gives people utterance to speak in tongues—an unphysical act to speak in heavenly mysteries to G-d in the Spirit as angels do vs. human languages, born out of Babel's sin of trying to be on G-d's level. Speaking and interpreting tongues are two spiritual gifts, but are only a sign for unbelievers, need interpretation and only build up the speaker.[99]

Triumphant Trumpet & Tree of Life

Shout to G-d in a **triumphant** voice! We are always led in a "triumphal procession" in Jesus. We will gloriously triumph over the enemy by the works of G-d's hands! Salvation! Oh sound, last **trumpet** 🎺 so we can rejoice with all our might in knowing the war is won. "The dead raised imperishable, and we will be changed," caught up to

---

[99] 2 Corinthians 13:14, Acts 2:4;17:30, 1 John 5:8, Matthew 23:8;28:19-20, Isaiah 6:3, Ecclesiastes 4:12, Psalms 31:15, Ephesians 1:10, Mark 13:32, James 3:1, John 14:26, 1 Corinthians 12:10;13:1;14:2;4;22, Hebrews 3:13

Jesus in a cloud. When the seventh angel trumpets, Jesus' reign will begin, and the mystery of G-d will be divulged.

Jesus is re-choosing the **Tree of Life** ♣, triumph over inescapable defeat. He fulfilled "cursed be the one who is hanged on a tree." Sin, the knowledge of good and evil, was nailed to the cross, along with the cursed law. After Jesus' return, the Tree of Life in the new Jerusalem will be in the middle of the river of living water, flowing from G-d's and Jesus' thrones. Jesus grants those remaining in Him the right to eat their share of the Tree of Life's twelve monthly fruits and healing leaves "in the paradise of G-d." Until then, wisdom, "a fruit of the righteous," "a soothing tongue," and a hopeful desire fulfilled are like a Tree of Life.[100]

---

[100] Psalms 20.5,4/:1;92:4, Revelation 2:7;8:2;10:7;11:15;22:1-2;14;19, 1 Corinthians 15:52, 1 Thessalonians 4:17 Proverbs 3:18;11:30;13:12;15:4

𝓤    u

Upright & Unchanging

G-d is strictly moral, reliable, and immune to evil. "Good and **upright** is Yahweh," such that no good is withheld from those who walk and speak with upright, blameless hearts in fear of G-d—rest, peace, light, sound wisdom, and seeing His face. G-d has perfect integrity. He is the same G-d millennia ago, as now, as for eternity. "No variation or shifting shadow." "For I, Yahweh, do not change; therefore, you, O children of Jacob, are not consumed." G-d's word will fully come to be. "The **unchangeableness** of His purpose, interposed with an oath" is to make us all His heirs, with Jesus our priest, who also is "the same yesterday and today and forever."[101]

United *Union*

Jesus has a mysterious ***union*** as "one flesh" with His *Church*, like *groom* and *bride* or head 👨 and body 👩. Be **united** in Jesus and His experience: suffering, death, and resurrection. Eagerly maintain unity in the Spirit—mind, thought, judgment, and love—in the bond of peace: one voice, heart, and soul in Jesus with no Church division.[102]

---

[101] Hebrews 6:17;7:21;13:8, Psalms 11:7;15:2;25:8;84:11;102:27;112:4, Isaiah 33:15;57:2; 1 Kings 3:6, Proverbs 2:7;14:2, James 1:17, Matthew 5:18, Malachi 3:6
[102] Ephesians 4:3-4, 1 Corinthians 1:10, Galatians 3:28, Philippians 2:2, Romans 6:5;15:6, Acts 4:32

Virtuous Vine

Jesus sets the bar with the highest moral standards of goodness—the **virtue** *virtuoso*. He always does G-d's will honorably, commendably, and excellently. Virtue is the first building block we are called to add to faith. We are to set our minds on anything virtuous or praiseworthy. Jesus says He is the true **Vine**, and G-d is the Vinedresser. "Abide in Me, and I in you. As the branch cannot bear fruit by itself, unless it abides in the Vine 🍇, neither can you, unless you abide in Me ... Whoever abides in Me and I in him, he will bear much fruit, for apart from Me you can do nothing." G-d removes the bad branches from Jesus and prunes the good ones so they can grow even more virtuous fruit. That is discipleship. Bear good fruit and not poisonous, bitter grapes from the vine of Sodom, or be cut down and burned. Jesus will not drink from the fruit of the vine until the day He can drink with us in our Father's kingdom![103]

Victorious Vindication

Yahweh fights our enemies and gives **victory**. "Death is swallowed up in victory." "O death, where is your victory? O death, where is your sting 🐝?" Faith is "the victor's

---

[103] John 15:1-8, Matthew 3:10;26:29, Deuteronomy 32:32-3, Philippians 4:8, 2 Peter 1:5

crown" over the world. "But thanks be to G-d, who gives us the victory through our Lord Jesus Christ!" G-d's people are **vindicated**—cleared of sin's blame —the only way to win.[104]

---

[104] Revelation 2:10, 1 Corinthians 15:57, Deuteronomy 20:4;32:36, 1 John 5:4, Hosea 13:14, Psalm 135:14

Washer

Baptism in the Trinity's names **washes** away sins: washed, sanctified, then justified in Jesus' name and by G-d's Spirit. Jesus washed feet, but now washes hands in innocence, bodies in pure water, and souls by His word. He sprinkles hearts clean of evil consciences. Believers' robes will be washed white in the Lamb's blood.[105]

Warrior

Yahweh is our mightiest **warrior**. Believers must put on G-d's full armor of light: the belt of truth; breastplate of righteousness; shoes of readiness from the gospel of peace; shield ♡ of faith; helmet of salvation; and sword ↘ of the Spirit, which is the word of G-d. Our weapons are not of flesh, but divine power. "Fight the good fight of faith" and be good soldiers for Jesus, who, when He returns atop a white horse, will righteously judge and war with His armies in heaven against the ultimate enemies, Satan and death, bringing final peace. Weapons will be turned into gardening tools, and war taught no more.[106]

---

[105] Acts 22:16, 1 Corinthians 6:11, Jeremiah 4:14, Hebrews 10:22, Revelation 7:14, Psalms 26:6, Exodus 15:3

[106] Ephesians 6:11-16, Exodus 15:3, Revelation 19:11-21, 1 Timothy 6:12, Zephaniah 3:17, 2 Corinthians 10:4, Isaiah 2:4, Romans 13:12

The Way, the Word & the Water

"Make ready the **way** of the Lord!" Yahweh's ways are higher than ours—the upright's stronghold is but iniquitous ruin by comparison. Know the way of holiness. Jesus said, "I am the way" to the Father. He inaugurated the new and living way with His flesh—the straightened path of righteousness, peace, and salvation back to the Tree of Life.

"In the beginning was the **Word**, and the Word was with G-d, and the Word was G-d." Abiding in the Word gives you all of this and more:

- † Power
- † The freeing truth
- † The good news' permanence
- † Blessings
- † The basis of faith
- † Hope
- † True discipleship
- † Healing
- † Spiritual sustenance
- † The all-discerning, sharpest double-edged sword of the Spirit
- † Life sustainment
- † Salvation or judgment
- † Guiding light
- † Wisdom
- † Instruction
- † Cleanliness
- † Purification
- † The door of opportunity opener
- † Training to be G-d's complete, approved workers, immortal heirs, and children

"G-d's word became flesh and dwelt among us." Jesus is the "author ✍ of life," who "upholds the universe by the word of His power." "In Him all things hold together." Immerse in the implanted, faithful word: sacred writings; G-d-breathed holy Scriptures; sound doctrine; and "pure spiritual milk 🥛." G-d's word cannot be changed or tampered with. Believers are like a "letter from Christ," "not written with ink but with the Spirit of the living G-d, not on tablets of stone, but on tablets of human hearts." "Your words were found, and I ate them, and your words became to me a joy and the delight of my heart, for I called you by name, O Yahweh, G-d of Hosts." Our words are also important: each will be accounted for; evil ones set the body aflame.

"Whoever believes in me, as the Scripture has said, 'out of his heart will flow rivers of living **water**.'" G-d's kingdom is only for those "born of water and the Spirit." Draw water from the well of salvation. Drink Jesus' free, living water and never thirst, having an internal spring welling up to eternal life.[107]

Willed for Works & Wisdom

G-d's **will** for Jesus is not to lose anyone G-d gave Him—His believers—but to raise them up on the last day to eternal life. "I have come to do your will, my G-d." Right before His crucifixion, Jesus prayed, "Abba, Father, all things are possible for you. Remove this cup from me. Yet, not what I will, but what You will." G-d's will was Jesus' food. G-d's intent for us in Jesus is known because the Spirit intercedes in His saints: "Rejoice always, pray continually, give thanks in all circumstances"; be sanctified and useful by abstaining from sexual immorality; and "put to silence the ignorance of foolish people." We can test for G-d's "good, pleasing, and perfect will." Doing G-d's will means G-d will listen to you, and you will become Jesus' brother or sister, and a receiver of G-d's promise—entering His kingdom.

Jesus answered G-d's calling in all of His **works**. "Now, there are also many other things that Jesus did. Were every one of them to be written, I suppose that the world itself could not contain the books that would be written." While

---

[107] Hebrews 1:3;4:12;10:20, 2 Timothy 2:15;3:15-17, Romans 1:1;15:4, James 1:21, 1 Peter 2:2, Jeremiah 15:16, Deuteronomy 4:2, 2 Corinthians 3:3, Colossians 1:17, John 1:1;14;3:5;7:38;8:32;14:6;15:3;17:17, Titus 1:9, Matthew 3:21;32;4:4;24:35, Isaiah 12:3;35:8;55:9, Acts 16:17, Proverbs 3:6;10:29, Luke 1:79;11:28, Psalms 107:20;119:105; 1 Corinthians 1:18, Revelation 22:1

only grace saves, believers are created in Jesus to be rich in and zealous for good works—Mitzvot. *Walking* in faith and good works are both needed to be justified. Good works bring faith to life and are pleasing sacrifices to G-d, but good works without faith are a stumbling stone, like the law. Always be abounding in Jesus' works. Never grow weary or give up on good works; the reaping will come "in due season." "Your labor is not in vain." Here is a partial list of good works: to believe in G-d, who sent Jesus; to let your light shine to give G-d glory; to thank G-d in everything; to obey the truth; to exhibit the fruits of the Spirit; and to "seek justice, correct oppression, bring justice to the fatherless, plead the widow's cause." Patiently seek glory, honor, and immortality with good works. Immersion in G-d's word equips "for every good work." Jesus' earthly work was carpentry, like His earthly dad Joseph's. Thank G-d for Jesus' final woodcraft 🪵! Whatever earthly work we do, it is to be done heartily for G-d, not man, in serving Jesus.

G-d's light will expose all works—good to life and bad to judgment. "For it is better to suffer for doing good, if that should be G-d's will, than for doing evil." It's a sin to know the right thing but not do it. Bad, unwise, and unfruitful works of flesh and darkness are of the world's or one's own will, not G-d's: to disobey the truth, obey unrighteousness, self-seek, or perform "sexual immorality, impurity, sensuality, idolatry, sorcery, enmity, strife, jealousy, fits of anger, rivalries, dissensions, divisions, envy, drunkenness, orgies ... anger, wrath, malice, slander, obscene talk," and deceit. Expose them!

"How manifold are your works, Yahweh! In **wisdom** have you made them all; the earth is full of your possessions." Spiritual wisdom—decreed before the ages—starts with the fear of G-d. Jesus became that "wisdom from G-d." G-d generously gives wisdom—understanding of His and Jesus' will and word. Just ask in faith. At end times, Jesus will give us the words of wisdom when we need to defend

Him. Wisdom is like pearls; don't throw yours at pigs 🐗. Wise people make the best use of their time; hold their tongues; hold hidden wisdom in their "secret hearts"; make the most out of each opportunity with outsiders; are slow to anger, cautious, and not wise in their own eyes; surround themselves with other wise people; and take advice. Humility is both a precursor and product of wisdom. Wisdom also produces these:

- † Honor
- † A loving life
- † Strength, with an uncuttable, soulful hope for the future
- † A long and good life filled with good deeds
- † A shining face
- † Judiciousness
- † Persuasiveness
- † Prosperity
- † Blessedness

"Wisdom from above is first pure, then peaceable, gentle, open to reason, full of mercy and good fruits, impartial, and sincere." Worldly, human wisdom is foolishness to G-d.[108]

Witness

Under the Law, two or more witnesses established the truth. Jesus is our faithful **witness**, who testifies for Himself, alongside His Father who sent Him. The Scriptures, the Holy Spirit, and disciples bear witness to

---
[108] Psalms 51:6;104:24, Galatians 5:19;6:9, Colossians 1:9;3:5-10;4:5-6;23-4, Mark 3:35;14:36, John 3:20;4:34;6:28-9;38-40;9:31;21:25, Romans 2:6-8;27;9:32;12:2, Ephesians 2:8-10;5:11;16;20, 1 Thessalonians 4:3;5:16-8; Hebrews 10:36;13:16, 1 Peter 2:15;3:17; James 1:5;2:17;24;3:13;4:17, Matthew 7:21, 1 Timothy 6:18, Titus 2:14, 2 Timothy 2:21;3:17, Isaiah 1:17, Proverbs 2:6;3;7;13-18;13;10,20;14:16;29;16:23;17:28;19:8;24:4;14, Luke 21:15, 1 Corinthians 1:30;2:7;3:19;15:58, Ecclesiastes 8:1

all Jesus did—that He was anointed by G-d to judge the living and the dead. At end times, two witnesses, "olive 🌿 trees," or "lampstands," will give testimony while bringing plagues, drought, and turning water to blood on earth. They will be raised to heaven after the beast kills them. The Holy Spirit empowers us to be witnesses locally, in our Jerusalem, Judea and Samaria, and to the earth's ends. When testimony is given across the earth to all nations, the end will come. Good witnesses shine their light, showing good works to give glory to the heavenly Father. The Holy Spirit bears witness with ours that we are G-d's children. Making good confession in the presence of many witnesses calls one to eternal life.[109]

Worthy & Wondrous

"**Worthy**, are You, our Lord and G-d, to receive glory and honor and power; for You created all things, and because of your will, they existed and were created." "Worthy is the Lamb who was slain, to receive power and wealth and wisdom and might and honor and glory and blessing!" "Worthy are You to take the scroll and open its seals, for You were slain, and by your blood You ransomed people for G-d from every tribe and language and people and nation. You have made them to be a kingdom and priests to serve G-d, and they will reign on earth"—lyrics that will be sung during Jesus' reign.

Jacob's humbled beautiful prayer to G-d: "I am not worthy of the least of all the deeds of steadfast love and all the faithfulness that You have shown to your servant." And, as John the Baptist said, we are not deserving of holding Jesus' sandal 👡. So, try to live your life worthy of Jesus, the gospel, and your calling by knowing G-d, keeping in repentance, bearing fruit in good works, standing firm

---

[109] Acts 1:8;5:32;10:42, John 5:39;8:17-8, Revelation 1:1-15, Matthew 5:16, Romans 8:16, 1 Timothy 6:12

in the Spirit, and striving side-by-side in faith. Keep your mind on what is worthy of praise, excellent, commendable, lovely, pure, just, honorable, and true. Those worthy of the age to come and in the resurrection from the dead will be like the angels, with neither marriage nor death. Find those with worthy hearts and spend time in their houses, letting your peace come upon them; but leave the company of the unworthy, and let your peace return to you. Elders who lead well, preach, and teach are worthy of double honor. Unworthiness is loving humans, even family, more than Jesus and not taking up your daily cross to follow Him.

G-d is worthy of praise for infinite reasons, including performing majestic splendors and awesome **wonders**. "Who is like You, O Yahweh, among the gods? Who is like You, majestic in holiness, awesome in glorious deeds, doing works?" "The heavens keep telling the wonders of G-d, and the skies declare what He has done." "Let all inhabitants of the world stand in awe of Him." When Jesus began performing miracles and healing, "everyone was gripped with great wonder and awe, and they praised G-d, exclaiming 'we have seen extraordinary things today!'" Everyone was also in awe when the apostles performed many wonders and signs through Jesus. Try to behold G-d and Jesus' wonder and awe; see the most astonishing, awesome, extraordinary things they do every day. But remember, Satan and his servants will also perform wonders to trick and deceive the world, including believers. So, hold fast to the word![110]

---

[110] Revelation 4:11;5:9-10;12, Philippians 1:27;4:8, Ephesians 4:1, Matthew 3:11;10:11;13;37-8, Colossians 1:10, Luke 3:8;20:35, 1 Timothy 5:17; Genesis 32:10, Exodus 15:11, Psalms 19:1;33:8, Acts 2:43

Xristos

The Greek word **Xristos**, from which "Christ" is derived, means "Anointed One" of G-d. The Messiah. Jesus is the only one with that title because Jesus was anointed in the Holy Spirit, not oil! Jesus was oathfully ordained by G-d to be every leader and hold every highest position:

- † Messiah
- † Savior
- † Lord of Glory
- † High Priest
- † King Lion
- † Prince of Peace
- † Prophet
- † Law-giver
- † Rabboni, Rabbi, Teacher, and Parable-Preacher
- † Mediator
- † Interceder and Advocate
- † Avenger
- † Firstborn
- † Head
- † Husband
- † Apostle and Messenger
- † Shepherd
- † G-d's only Son
- † Heir

Jesus is One-of-a-kind. Leadership roles were split amongst humans because they could not be done by one person. Now, Jesus is perfectly all of them for all time!

And yet He came as our friend, servant, sacrificial offering—Lamb. Fully divine, yet fully human. Son of G-d and Son of Man.

Christ Jesus! Xristos Iesous! Mashiach Yeshua! X-ristos marks the spot![111]

---

[111] Mark 1:1, Acts 10:38

Yahweh

Yahweh—the tetragrammaton for its four Hebrew letters YHVH—is a holy name, without proper pronunciation. Yahweh is Abraham's provider; Moses' banner, strength, song, and salvation; David's sun, light, tower, fortress, rock, strength and shield, shepherd, Mighty One, Deliverer, and salvation; Gideon's peace; Jeremiah's righteous savior and everlasting King; Ezekiel's sovereign; Zechariah's King; and Zephaniah's mighty warrior. Yahweh may be the Father or Jesus, or a combination of the Trinity. Perhaps that will be included when all mysteries are revealed, along with Jesus' experience in the OT, after end times. What we do know is that Jesus was called G-d and works in perfect unison with G-d and the Holy Spirit, from before the ages, to now, and on to eternity.[112]

Yeshua

The OT was written in Aramaic-Hebrew, and Jesus' name is **Yeshua**, meaning "salvation." Jacob, Moses, Job, Hannah, David, Isaiah, Jeremiah, Jonah, and Micah all used this root. "No longer will violence be heard in your land, neither wasting nor destruction within your borders, but you will

---

[112] Genesis 22:4, Jeremiah 10:10;23:6, Judges 6:24, Psalms 18:31;23:1;27:1;28:7;50:1, 2 Samuel 22:2, Zechariah 14:9

call your walls Yeshua, 'salvation,' and your gates Tehillah, 'prayer.'" Yeshua's *yoke* is easy because He saved us from the "yoke of slavery," which is death.[113]

---

[113] Isaiah 52:7;60:18, Exodus 14:13;15:2, Job 13:16, 1 Samuel 2:1, Psalms 25:5, Genesis 49:18, Micah 7:7, Jeremiah 17:14, Jonah 2:9, Galatians 5:1, Matthew 11:30

Zealous ... for Zion

G-d is **zealous** for His holy name. He stirs up His zeal like a warrior, wearing it like a cloak. Yahweh of Hosts' zeal brought these prophecies: "Out of Jerusalem shall go a remnant, and out of Mount **Zion** a band of survivors"; "For us, a child is born"; and "His government and of peace there will be no end." It was "zeal for [G-d's] house, which consumed" Jesus because Jesus' body is G-d's temple.

Jesus' redemption and purification + our zeal for good works = G-d's possession.

"Don't be slothful in zeal, but fervent in spirit, serve the Lord." Don't be zealous for knowledge or fathers' traditions. Be zealous in the Father's zeal, seeking citizenship in heaven.

G-d is jealous for Jerusalem, and zealous for Zion—"fortified *zenith*," or "signpost" in Hebrew. The fear of Yahweh is Zion's treasure. Zion is a hill in Jerusalem, but metaphysically is the city of Yahweh, "the Holy One of Israel"; G-d's "holy mountain" and chosen dwelling, with Jesus as its cornerstone and King; the living G-d's gated city; heavenly Jerusalem; and Eden. It is the source of the law, the word, and salvation, where thousands upon thousands of angels are in joyful assembly. Zion is the "church of the Firstborn [Jesus], whose names are written in heaven." The Lamb will stand atop Mount Zion with His 144,000 undefiled "firstfruits" redeemed from earth, the only ones to know Jesus' new song, who will go wherever He goes.[114]

---

[114] Ezekiel 39:25, Titus 2:14, Isaiah 2:3;9:6-7;28:16;33:6;42:13;51:3;59:17;60:14, Romans 10:2;12:11 Revelation 3:19;14:1-4, Psalms 14:769:9;87:2;132:13-4, John 2:17-22, Galatians 1:14, Numbers 25:13, Joel 3:17, Hebrews 12:22-3, Zechariah 9:9, Philippians 3:20

A to Z

Nothing replaces G-d's Holy Word in the Bible, the basis of this book. This book doesn't even capture the tip of the iceberg 🧊 of their greatness. Books could fill the world with their praise and fall infinitely short. G-d, Jesus, and the Holy Spirit span all time, languages, and quite literally A to Z, Alpha to Omega. Amen.

I leave you with one of my favorite quotes from Scripture:

"For I am sure that neither death nor life, nor angels nor rulers, nor things present nor things to come, nor powers, nor height nor depth, nor anything else in all of creation, will be able to separate us from the love of G-d in Christ Jesus our Lord." - Romans 8:38-39

www.ingramcontent.com/pod-product-compliance
Ingram Content Group UK Ltd.
Pitfield, Milton Keynes, MK11 3LW, UK
UKHW060124240426
12049UKWH00012B/154